ALANNAH MOORE

CREATE
YOUR OWN
WEBSITE

THE *Easy Way*

ilex

An Hachette UK Company
www.hachette.co.uk

First published in Great Britain in 2016 by
ILEX, a division of Octopus Publishing Group Ltd

Octopus Publishing Group
Carmelite House
50 Victoria Embankment
London, EC4Y 0DZ
www.octopusbooks.co.uk

Design, layout, and text copyright
© Octopus Publishing Group 2016

Publisher: Roly Allen
Commissioning Editor: Zara Larcombe
Editor: Rachel Silverlight
Managing Specialist Editor: Frank Gallaugher
Senior Project Editor: Natalia Price-Cabrera
Art Director: Julie Weir
Designers: Anders Hanson and Ginny Zeal
Production Controller: Marina Maher

ISBN 978-1-78157-290-0

A CIP catalogue record for this book is available
from the British Library

Printed and bound in China

10 9 8 7 6 5 4 3 2 1

Introduction

WHY CREATE *your own* WEBSITE?

Until just a few years ago, if you wanted to make your own website, you'd have to learn web design.

Of course, even this wasn't actually a very good solution. Making websites is a complicated business and it takes a lot of practice. You also need a good deal of knowledge, not to mention being skilled at design as well, to get something that looks really good. It is vital that your website does look good because it is the public face of your business—or in the case of a personal website, it's your own, individual, face that is now open to public display.

Today, though, the world of website creation is entirely different. A whole spectrum of different website-building platforms has evolved that enable people to create their own websites without any special technical knowledge.

You just need clarity of purpose, and varying amounts of time to dedicate to it, depending on what you want to achieve and the platform you choose to work on.

The advantages of creating your own website are obvious.

- You can control the site yourself. This means that you can project the exact image you want to your public, without needing to convey your vision to your web designer.

- You can update it. You can add blog posts, update the website content, and add products and change prices; your website needs to be up to date, and besides, Google loves content that is updated regularly.

- You can tweak it as often as you like. You can adjust the text to improve your rankings in Google, or test responses from your prospective clients.

- It's much more convenient. You don't have to wait for your busy web designer to schedule the updates—you can just do them whenever you like.

- Finally, you can save a large amount of money if you handle your website yourself.

What this book will not teach you

This book is not about coding. In fact, instead of teaching you about coding, this book aims to show you how to avoid learning any coding at all. (Not that there is anything wrong with coding—this book is just for people who do other things!)

Unfortunately, this book cannot teach you how to do everything. Not absolutely every idea you might conceivably have for your website can be accomplished using one of the easy-to-use website-building platforms. If you want something very specific, it could be that your idea is so original that there just isn't an ready-made tool that will allow you to set it up yourself without seeking the advice of a professional. If you don't find a way of doing what you want to do in this book, do some research on Google; things develop very fast in the world of the web and amazing new tools do become available all the time. But if your research proves fruitless, this means it is time to call on a specialist who can work with you to bring your idea to fruition.

Good luck creating your fabulous website.

Keep up to date
Click over to my website to keep up to date with the latest tools available for you to use. Feel free to ask questions! I'll answer them on my blog, if I feel other readers would benefit as well.

HTTP://WWW.ALANNAHMOORE.COM

1 Before *You Start*

Can anyone CREATE *their own* WEBSITE?

Before we get into details of planning out your new website, let's start off with some of the basics, and cover some general advice that you can keep in your mind as you progress.

In the past I actually dissuaded people from building their own websites for the reasons I talked about in the introduction. I used to advise people to stay away, hire a professional, and spend their precious time working on their business instead!

But there is now such a range of platforms (different systems) that you can use to create a website yourself, without getting into any complex coding or design, that really anyone can create a website that looks absolutely, perfectly professional.

There are two keys to pulling off the self-built website successfully. The first is choosing a platform that is suitable for you. If you're not confident fiddling around on your computer, don't choose self-hosted WordPress, for example. A simpler system such as Strikingly or Weebly will give you something that looks just as good, with far less work behind it.

The second key is knowing where to draw the line. It is amazing that so many wonderful platforms exist that let people sidestep the coding process completely. But, as I said in the introduction, not everything you want to do can always be done without coding. If you want to do something complex, realize that you may be taking the project out of the do-it-yourself arena.

DEAL PLATFORMS

WordPress.org

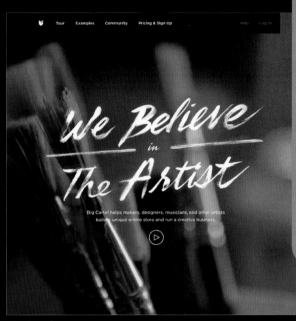

Big Cartel

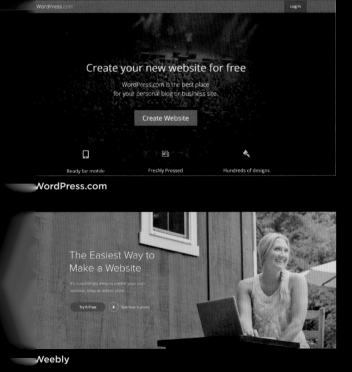

WordPress.com

Weebly

Shopify

Strikingly

Before you BEGIN

Starting-out Advice for the DIY Website Builder

FOLLOW THIS ADVICE TO STEER CLEAR OF THE MOST COMMON PITFALLS

- Realize that you're better off building your site entirely yourself, using one of the simpler DIY systems, than getting a techie friend to help you with a more complicated system. You'll kick yourself if you can't work out how to make changes on your website yourself, and are obliged to chase your friend every time you want to change something.

- You may know a well-meaning young person studying web design who will offer to help you with your website to "get experience." Not only will that young person most likely be off on a more important project in no time at all, but it's also very likely they are not experienced or knowledgeable in anything to do with marketing or your field of business. So consider whether this is really a good person to help you.

- Don't hesitate over whether or not you should get your own domain name. (A domain name is a website address that looks like this: "http://www.mywebsite.com".) This goes for personal sites as well as professional ones; a domain name is inexpensive, and easy to register—so get yourself one and look as though you mean business.

- Never let anyone else "help" you by registering your domain name for you under their own name; similarly, don't let anyone else host the site for you. You need to have control yourself of your domain name and (if applicable) your hosting—it's a big risk to let anyone else take charge of these.

- Just as you need a proper domain name in order to look serious, do pay whatever sum is asked to remove ads or branding from your site—they just make your website look messy and amateurish.

- Only alter the look of a pre-designed template if you are confident you have a good eye for design. This is a big danger area for non-designers, so don't let yourself down by letting the temptation to change things get the better of you.

SEVEN GRAMS CAFFÉ
WIX

| USA | HTTP://WWW.SEVENGRAMSCAFFE.COM |

"When building a website, you need to think carefully about the purpose of the website before creating it. It is this aspect that should guide your choices, both for design and content.

Many brick-and-mortar businesses that don't have an e-commerce side pay a lot of attention to their physical sites and slightly disregard their online presence. They tend to forget that many people check out your website in order to make a decision whether to visit your store or not, and if your website is lackluster, you might be losing business without even knowing it.

Treat the website like a genuine extension of your physical presence and to apply the same methodology you would to modeling your retail store. This would mean that first of all, you need to define the purpose of your website—for us it was to entice people to visit our physical store.

I devoted time to define the vision for the website—thinking of the categories I wanted featured, drawing a draft of the look and feel, collecting inspiration images from magazines and other websites, and outlining the values I wanted to convey. Once I had a clear vision, finding a food stylist, food photographer, and graphic designer that would be able to translate that vision into online reality was key. It was just as important as finding the right architect and interior designer for our retail store.

Balance your vision with knowing what you're not good at and look for people who can fill those gaps."

Sharon Kazes

What kind of WEBSITE do you want to SET UP?

Before you launch into any kind of decision-making about how to move forward with your self-built site, you need first to be clear on what kind of website it is that you want to set up.

Is your website going to be:
- A blog?
- An online portfolio?
- An online store?
- A simple online presence for your business, with contact details?
- A personal branding site?
- A sales page for a specific product?
- A page to collect email addresses?

Or is it a hybrid? Many—perhaps most—sites are in fact hybrids. Yours might be:
- Primarily a simple online presence, but with a blog attached giving news updates about what you're working on.
- A portfolio of your work, with a blog to show some of your sketches and behind-the-scenes details of your design process, or things that catch your eye.
- A blog with a store attached (or the other way around).
- A brochure site with a sales page attached for people to sign up for workshops.
- A brochure site with a blog and a store and means of collecting email addresses from the site visitors.

Being clear on the kind of website you are going to create will be essential for the planning process.

△ **Design blog Decor8 inspires and delights its visitors. It also acts as a platform for creator Holly Becker, pointing visitors to her books, and to the separate website on which people can sign up for online courses. HTTP://DECOR8BLOG.COM**

Design and layout: Solo Pine Designs (http://solopine.com); Mark Wilson (www.mwadesign.com); and Thorsten Becker (https://twitter.com/alternatewords); logo: Corinna Nika (http://www.cocorrina.com/)

WHAT PURPOSE WILL
YOUR WEBSITE SERVE?

It's also really important to realize what purpose, or purposes, you mean your website to serve for you—in order to make sure it does fulfill its function.

Your website could:

- Present you as an expert.
- Inform, inspire, and entertain your visitors.
- Showcase your work.
- Capture interested people's email addresses.
- Sell your products.
- State what you do and provide an online point of contact.

...or several of these.

△ A humorous and lively example of a personal branding site.
HTTP://NATHANROBERTSON.STRIKINGLY.COM

◁ Dowse Design is an online store for a design studio with a blog attached. The blog updates customers on latest news and also includes photos, interviews, and design guides.
HTTP://DOWSEDESIGN.CO.UK

Choosing a DOMAIN NAME

Your domain name is your address on the internet, for example **"http://www.mywebsite. com."** As I've mentioned, whatever kind of website you are building, whether it's personal or professional, you really do need your own domain name, rather than using the free website address given to you by your chosen platform. But how do you choose the right domain name?

◁ The extension or "TLD" (top-level domain) is the part at the end of the domain name.

BRANDING OR A SEARCH TERM?

The first thing to ask yourself is, how important is branding to you? If you want people to remember you by your own name or by your business name, then you want a domain name that matches. (If you haven't yet named your business, you might want to research a suitable, matching, and available domain name at the same time.)

If distinguishing yourself from others via your branding isn't that important to you, which may well be the case if you run a local service business and are aiming to attract customers via the search engines, you might want to choose a keyword or phrase instead for you domain name. Try the combination of your town or area plus your keyword (such as "dentist" or "design")—that's how most people will probably search for you.

Note that this will not necessarily guarantee a flood of visitors finding you via the search engines, but it is one factor that Google takes into consideration when deciding how to rank your website (we'll talk more about keywords and search engines in Chapter 11). Examples of this type of domain name would be huntingdonplumber.com or brightondoctor. co.uk—or cambridge-dentist.co.uk, which you can see in the screenshot on the facing page.

SHOULD YOU BUY THE OTHER VERSIONS OF YOUR DOMAIN NAME— .NET, .CO.UK, ETC.?

To protect your brand, and stop anyone else buying them, you might want to secure the versions of your domain name with other extensions, plus also hyphenated versions, misspellings, etc. How far you go with this is up to you.

WHEN YOU'RE CHOOSING YOUR DOMAIN NAME:

- You might wish to avoid hyphens. There isn't a hard-and-fast rule about this, but they tend to cause confusion as people can forget them.
- Don't make it hard to spell.
- Don't make it too long.
- Be sure it isn't going to conflict with anyone else's business or trademark.

▽ Two different approaches—one domain name is chosen for search engine purposes, the other because the brand is more important.
HTTP://CAMBRIDGE-DENTIST.CO.UK
HTTP://ELKUS-MANFREDI.COM

Cambridge
Dentist

24/7 Cambridge
Emergency Dental Service
07973 227 415

Surgery Appointments
7 Days A Week
01223 363277

1d Brooke House, Kingsley Walk, Newmarket Road, Cambridge, CB5 8TJ.

Reception@cambridgedentalcare.co.uk

Our Team   Fees   Location   News   Special Offers   Your first Visit   Opening Hours   Contact   Staying Ahead

Cambridge Dentist
Practice
Open Every Day
Every Week

Cambridge
Emergency Dentist
Is Available 24/7
365 days a year

The New Cambridge Dentist Practice

ELKUS | MANFREDI
ARCHITECTS

CIVIC | PUBLIC
HIGHER EDUCATION
HOSPITALITY | DINING
INTERNATIONAL
OFFICE BUILDINGS
PLANNING | MIXED-USE
PRESERVATION
RESIDENTIAL
RETAIL | ENTERTAINMENT
SCIENCE + TECHNOLOGY
WORKPLACE INTERIORS
OUR FIRM

WHICH EXTENSION TO CHOOSE?

Until recently, your choice of TLD was very limited. There was basically .com, .net, .org and .info together with the country-specific extensions like .co.uk, .com.au, .ca, .fr, etc. (also known as "ccTLDs").

This made it quite hard to find a good domain name that wasn't already taken. Now there are a host of new extensions to choose from, such as .restaurant, .kitchen, .agency, .boutique, .dance, .health, .fitness, .music, .photography, .art, .design, .life, .website, .cooking, .garden, .dentist, .plumbing, .doctor, .architect .nyc, or .london—and that's just a few. There are literally hundreds now available, and new ones becoming available all the time. While they are more expensive than your regular .com domain name, you might consider it worth the expense to bag yourself a great web address.

IS THE DOMAIN NAME YOU WANT AVAILABLE?
Don't just Google the domain name you want to see if it is available—often you'll find the domain has been bought, but not used! Instead, search availability via a registrar such as Namecheap.com or GoDaddy.com.

▷ Hundreds of new domain name extensions are now available, as shown here on the Namecheap.com website (click "New TLDs" from the menu).

.COM OR A COUNTRY-SPECIFIC EXTENSION?
Use a country-specific extension if you want to indicate that you don't plan to do business with international clients. This might be the case if you run a service business that's specific to your area, for which your clients are necessarily local, or if you don't ship your products globally.

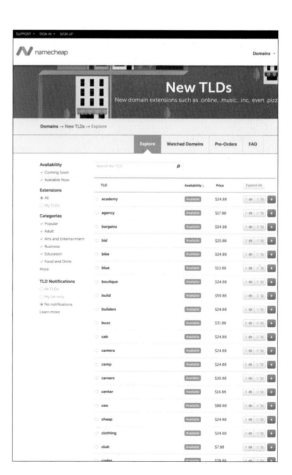

GETTING CREATIVE WITH YOUR DOMAIN NAME

There's loads of fun to be had choosing a domain name—see the examples on this page—if you feel like getting creative. Two brilliant tools to come up with good domain names are Domainr.com and NameMesh.com which you can see in the screenshots below; based on what you type into the search box, they come up with a stream of suggestions and alternatives, drawing on country-specific TLDs as well as the new extensions.

Other ideas for original domain names include using slogans or part of a phrase or sentence (but don't make it too long), changing spellings (like Dribbble), or totally inventing words (try wordoid.com to come up with some good ones)—it's hard to think back that far, but Google was once a made-up word!

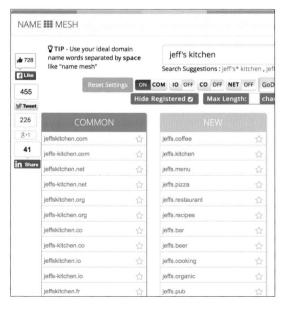

◁ △ **NameMesh and Domainr are brilliant tools for coming up with a fun and creative domain name.**
HTTP://WWW.NAMEMESH.COM
HTTP://DOMAINR.COM

Registering your DOMAIN NAME

Once you've chosen your domain name, you need to register it. Registration is done by the year but you may want to "purchase" a few years at once to save yourself having to renew each year.

WHERE TO REGISTER YOUR DOMAIN NAME

It may be that the platform you choose will offer to sell you a domain name through them. This is certainly the most straightforward solution, and you may be tempted to go this way simply to make life easier, but actually, I wouldn't advise it. If you later want to change system, you will find you need to move the registration of the domain name to an independent registrar, and while this will always be possible, figuring it out may take some time and is more or less guaranteed to give you a headache.

Instead I recommend you register with a reliable independent registrar such as Namecheap.com, GoDaddy.com, or any of the options in the box to the right, which frees you up to make whatever decision you like, at any time further down the line.

REPUTABLE DOMAIN NAME REGISTRARS

You may want to do your own research before choosing a registrar to check its reliability. These are some of the most popular:

- Namecheap
- GoDaddy
- HostGator
- eNom
- 1&1
- Hover
- Name.com

Note that your domain name registrar doesn't have to be in the same country as you.

CONNECTING YOUR DOMAIN TO YOUR PLATFORM

Once you've registered your domain name, the system you choose will let you know what you need to do to connect up your new domain name. (The exception to this is of course if you're using self-hosted WordPress, because you'll need your own hosting company to host your website. We'll come to this a little later.)

Connecting your domain name to your chosen platform will involve changing the "nameserver" settings in the admin area of your registrar's website (also referred to as "DNS," which simply stands for "domain name system"). Once you've made the changes, you'll normally need to wait a few hours before the new domain is connected to your website-building system. (You can usually begin working on it while you're waiting.)

If you feel this is sounding a little too techie before you've even done anything, don't be dismayed. Your platform will give you very precise instructions as to how this is done, and will always help you if needed. Feel free to skip this part for now and come back to it when you've chosen your platform, planned your website, and are ready to get going.

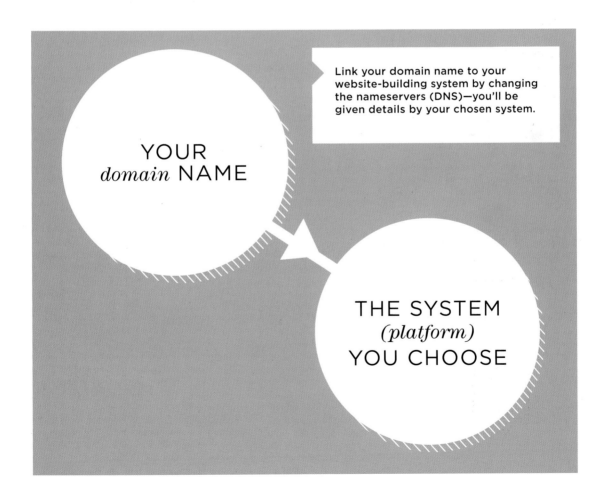

Link your domain name to your website-building system by changing the nameservers (DNS)—you'll be given details by your chosen system.

YOUR *domain* NAME

THE SYSTEM *(platform)* YOU CHOOSE

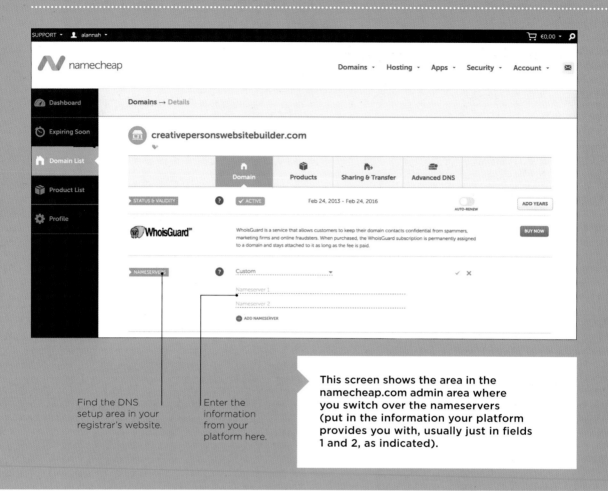

Find the DNS setup area in your registrar's website.

Enter the information from your platform here.

This screen shows the area in the namecheap.com admin area where you switch over the nameservers (put in the information your platform provides you with, usually just in fields 1 and 2, as indicated).

LOOKING AFTER YOUR DOMAIN

It's important to register your domain name with an email address you use regularly; you will receive renewal reminders sent to this email address only, and you really don't want to miss them. It's also a good idea to make a recurring reminder in a calendar of the date you need to renew your domain name.

Don't let your domain lapse. You may be able to get it back for a short while after it lapses, as the registrar may safeguard it for you, but it's not worth taking any risks!

REGISTERING COUNTRY-SPECIFIC DOMAINS

The cost of registering a country-specific extension can vary considerably from registrar to registrar so you'll certainly want to compare prices.

YASMINE DAILY
SELF-HOSTED WORDPRESS

SWITZERLAND | HTTP://YASMINEDAILY.COM

> When building a website, you need to think carefully about the purpose of the website before creating it. It is this that should guide your choices, both for design and content.
>
> It is important to research what your competitors are doing in your field, to find an angle that has not yet been treated ... or do what they are doing, better than them!
>
> You shouldn't be too concerned about spending money to create your website. Buying a premium theme, for example, will help you have a nicer looking and fully functional website, so it's definitely money well spent.
>
> My website was a way for me to assert myself in my profession—I'm a visual communication designer. Since I launched my website in early 2015, I found a job and now have a community behind me. Creating a website—especially a blog—allows us to share what we love with people, and forces us to do research, which enriches us day after day.

Created by Yasmine Moura

Choosing your HOSTING

Your domain name is your address on the internet, and your hosting is the space you rent to build your website. You purchase this from a hosting company, which is also known as a web host.

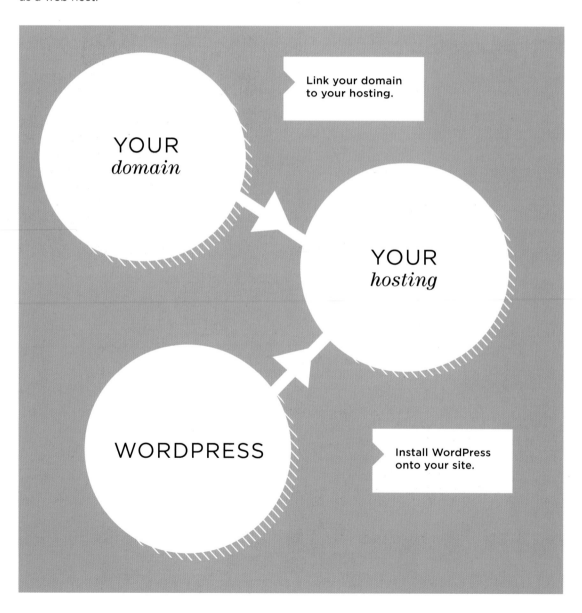

DO YOU NEED HOSTING?

While you'll need a domain name whichever system you choose to build your website on, you only need to get your own hosting if you're going to use self-hosted WordPress.* So if you're not going to use self-hosted WordPress, you can happily ignore this section.

Your domain name registrar may well offer you hosting, and the other way round as well, and you may find this more convenient, but I recommend that you get a host that is separate from your domain name registrar; specialist hosting companies are usually better, but this is, of course, your decision.

*There are some other "open source"—i.e. free—software systems you could use, such as Drupal or Joomla!, for which you'd also need to get your own hosting, but I don't recommend either of those as an easily do-able DIY option.

To host your WordPress site, your hosting company needs to fulfill the following criteria:

- It should offer an easy way of installing WordPress. You might see this described as a "one-click" install or an "easy install" system—just ask if in any doubt. This is important because if they don't, you'll have to install WordPress manually, and that's not something a beginner will want to do.
- It needs to be capable of running PHP and MySQL—these are the requirements for hosting a WordPress site.
- You need to be able to contact them 24/7, and so much the better if there's a phone number you can call or an online chat.
- They need to have a good "uptime" record—that's to say, their servers are almost never down (you're looking for 99 or 100%).
- Your hosting company should ideally be based in the same country as you, as Google prefers this.

SHARED HOSTING

For most people, a "shared" hosting package is all that you need. Of course, it depends on what your project is, and if you are in any doubt as to whether you need a more sophisticated package, ask the hosting company. But for the vast majority of cases, a shared hosting package will be sufficient, and there's no need to go for anything more expensive. ("Shared" hosting simply means that your site will be residing on a server with other users, but you will never be aware of them or experience that you are sharing anything.)

MORE HOSTING CONSIDERATIONS

You may also want to consider the following:

- Does your host offer you unlimited email addresses, should you need them for other people working with you in your business?
- Does your host offer you unlimited storage, if you want to store a large number of images or other heavy files on your site?
- Does your host offer you unlimited bandwidth, in case you get a stampede of traffic?
- Does your host offer you more than one database, in case you want to build any more WordPress websites?
- Can it host an unlimited number of domain names?

CONNECTING YOUR DOMAIN TO YOUR HOSTING

Your hosting company will usually be able to register domains for you, and will often encourage you to do this by offering you a free domain name for your first year, included in your hosting package. I suggest that you don't go for this option and register your domain separately from an independent registrar (see the box on page 18). This allows you complete flexibility, supposing you need to move your site at any point.

When you have your hosting package set up, you need to connect it with your domain by logging in to your domain name registrar's site and putting in the nameserver information the hosting package provides you with, as shown on pages 18–20.

RECOMMENDED HOSTS

- WP Engine (https://wpengine.com)
- Bluehost (https://www.bluehost.com)
- DreamHost (https://www.dreamhost.com)
- SiteGround https://www.siteground.com)
- Heart Internet (https://www.heartinternet.uk)

Before taking out a hosting package, do some research on Google and check that the host you are considering has recent good reviews.

Note that hosting companies often offer special deals for the first year or two, but you need to read the small print to work out what the price will be once your introductory period is over.

THE MUTTON CLUB
SELF-HOSTED WORDPRESS

| UK | HTTP://WWW.THEMUTTONCLUB.COM |

> "**F**ind a website you like and model yours on theirs. It's not about copying, but it's easier to take inspiration from a site you like, rather than trying to design one from scratch.
>
> I started off using web designers, both of whom I found online. But I was too trusting of knowledge levels and references on the site. So I finally decided to do it myself, and built a rudimentary new site in a day!
>
> A good hosting company will make life so much easier. I thought my host WP Engine would just deal with hosting issues. Instead they have helped me with any WordPress issues. They're not cheap, but having their support team on the end of the phone 24/7 helped enormously.
>
> When choosing which plugins to use, Google which are best for the job you need. **"**

Rachel Lankester

Taking payment ONLINE

If you intend to sell products online, you're going to need a means of collecting payment on your website.

The very simplest way of taking payment is via PayPal (customers can also pay by credit or debit card via the PayPal interface). Most platforms can work with PayPal and it's extremely convenient.

If you plan to make sales in any kind of quantity though, you will probably want to evolve to a different third-party payment system for the majority of your payments in order to reduce the fees you have to pay per transaction. Different systems allow for different payment processors; Stripe, WebMoney, Skrill, 2Checkout, Authorize.Net, Sage Pay, and PAYMILL being among those that may be offered.

Shopify offers you a "point-of-sale" credit card reader so you can accept payments using an iPad or smartphone via your Shopify store at fairs, trade shows and conferences.

HTTP://WWW.SHOPIFY.COM/POS

Square is a way of taking payment via credit and debit card in real-world situations, which you can now integrate with your Weebly, Squarespace or self-hosted WordPress website as a simple way of taking payment online as well. (At the time of writing, Square isn't yet available globally.)

HTTPS://SQUAREUP.COM

Before you decide on your platform, make sure the system works with a payment processor that you can use depending on where you're based, and make sure you check whether there is a setup fee as well as the usual per-transaction fee.

PAYMENT OPTIONS

Make it as easy as possible for your customers to buy from you. If you can, offer different ways of collecting payment; PayPal, credit/debit card, and potentially, if any of these work for you, check, payment on delivery, or bank transfer.

Above: **Unna Birch uses Big Cartel to sell her cookery book.**

HTTP://WWW.THEFORESTCANTINA.COM

Right: **Tasty Art sells food art via the Shopify platform.** (Design: Duke Mettle)

HTTP://WWW.TASTYART.CO.UK

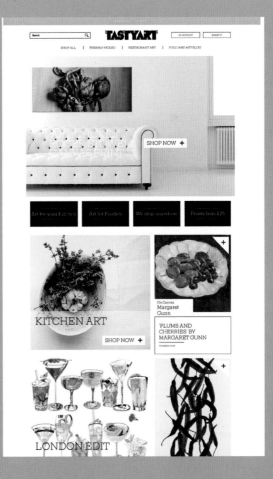

2 Your *Platform*

Choosing your PLATFORM

In this chapter we'll look at some of the best options available to today's website builder. A platform is simply a system that is used for building a website. While the platform isn't in itself the most important thing, the platform you choose can enable you or constrain you, or make the website-building process needlessly difficult. It's therefore a massively important decision.

There are loads of options you can choose from to build your website. Exciting new systems are being developed all the time, so if you find one not mentioned in this book that fits your needs, don't overlook it because you don't see it talked about here. If it has all the features you need, and looks the way you want it to look, then it may well be a great choice for you.

CHECKING OUT A SHOWCASE
Most platforms have a showcase allowing you to see examples of live sites built using that platform. While this gives you a great idea of what can potentially be done, be careful, as some of the websites on show may have been built with the help of a professional. In general, it's better to look at the templates (sometimes called themes) instead to properly understand what you can do by yourself.

How do you choose which platform to go with? These are the major considerations to take into account:

1. First of all, what features do you need? For example, do you need a blog, or a built-in portfolio? Make sure the system you choose can fulfill the purpose of your website, and has all the features you need, both now and in the foreseeable future.

2. How do the templates look? Appearance is seriously important. Your site can portray you as serious, or a dabbler, depending on the image you convey. So if the templates of a certain system just don't look right for you, steer away from that system.

3. Do you want to sell online? If so, check what payment systems the platform accepts, and how e-commerce works on sites built with that platform. (In addition, if you are planning to sell digital downloads such as e-books, you need to check if the platform has a facility for this.)

4. Will your website be mobile-friendly, with the smartphone view matching the desktop design? (See the next page.)

5. Does the platform suit your ability level? For instance, self-hosted WordPress is a more complicated choice than using a "hosted" system (such as Weebly or Wix).

6. Is there a free trial period that allows you to play around with the system and find out whether it is going to work for you?

▷ Browsing templates helps you get a good idea of what you could create yourself. Seen here, some Weebly templates, some Shopify templates, and some of the WordPress themes (templates) you can purchase from Dessign (https://dessign.net)— just one of the many providers of beautiful-looking WordPress themes.

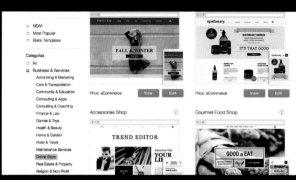

Weebly

PREMIUM RESPONSIVE WORDPRESS THEMES

BUY OVER 115+ PREMIUM THEMES FOR ONLY $99 – LIFETIME MEMBERSHIP
TRUSTED BY 85,000+ USERS

WordPress

Shopify

MOBILE-FRIENDLY *sites*

With mobile internet use equaling, if not outstripping, desktop surfing, there's no question that your new website needs to look good on mobile. You don't want your site visitors to have to scroll from left to right or read really tiny text; that makes for a really uncomfortable browsing experience. In addition, did you know that Google now favors websites that work well on mobile, over those that don't?

The good news is that most platforms provide you with a "mobile-friendly" version of your website that shows automatically to visitors surfing from their mobile, and some platforms even allow you to adjust this layout to be sure it appears as you'd like it to for viewers visiting your site via their phone.

Note that with some site-builders there may be "a mobile-optimized version" which looks good on mobiles but doesn't look the same as the design you created for desktop; the ideal is, of course, a mobile site that matches the look of the desktop version. So check carefully when choosing both platform and template (the wording may change from platform to platform so it's best to check their examples).

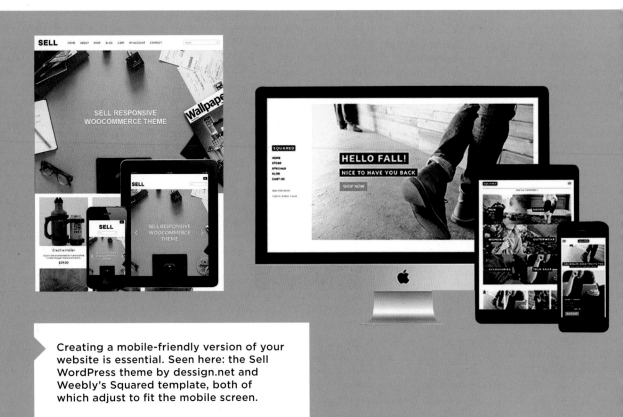

Creating a mobile-friendly version of your website is essential. Seen here: the Sell WordPress theme by dessign.net and Weebly's Squared template, both of which adjust to fit the mobile screen.

If you're building your website using WordPress, the key is to look for a theme (template) that's described as "responsive"—this means the elements adjust to fit the size of the smaller screen, with the look of the site remaining the same—as you can see in the examples (below left). Don't just assume they will be responsive —older templates may not be.

▷ In order for Google to class your website as "mobile-friendly," the website content has to adjust to fit the screen of your smartphone.

All Strikingly's templates are responsive. Seen here: Bright template.

There are blogs on WordPress.com covering every conceivable subject. It's really easy for you to set up a blog using their system—but making the blog your own with your distinctive photos, graphics and writing is what brings it to life and keeps your readers visiting.

Top: **HTTP://MYCUSTARDPIE.COM**
Bottom: **HTTP://BESPOKETRAVELER.COM**

WORDPRESS

HTTPS://WWW.WORDPRESS.COM
HTTPS://WWW.WORDPRESS.ORG

WordPress is an extremely popular choice for people building their own websites. In fact, it's so popular that a quarter of all websites in existence run on WordPress. Before we go any further, let's be very clear on one thing: there are two kinds of WordPress you can use to build your website.

The first, "WordPress.com," is a system that is hosted for you. This means that you don't have to set up your own hosting account and install the software. It's all done for you; but the downside is that you are limited in what you can do with your website. You can't add extras to it (called "plugins," see page 34) and you have to choose from the templates (called "themes") they make available to you, rather than having the massive choice of all the WordPress themes available to buy from independent developers. You can see the full list of pros and cons on page 35, but it breaks down to one thing, basically: don't choose WordPress.com if you want to set up any other kind of website other than a blog. If you do want to create a blog, however, it's the best hosted choice there is.

The other kind of WordPress site is the "self-hosted" version known as "WordPress.org." This is the same system as hosted WordPress.com, but it has many more options. To build your website with it, you need to set up your own hosting account and install WordPress. Once installed, you work on your website through your internet browser (Firefox, Safari, etc.). Self-hosted WordPress is suitable for whatever kind of site you want to build, whether it's a blog or a different kind of site: an online store, a portfolio, and so on; for both types of WordPress, you will be using a pre-designed template to build your website.

BENJAMINE MORRISON
SELF-HOSTED WORDPRESS

FRANCE

HTTP://WWW.BENJAMINEMORRISON.COM

> "My biggest challenge was initially finding a WordPress theme that met all of my practical and aesthetic requirements. Once I had found a theme, I had to become familiar with the WordPress interface and lingo, which were not initially intuitive for me. There was a bit of a learning curve but now I'm hooked and want to learn more. Thankfully, there is a large and growing community of WordPress users, so plenty of support can be found online.
>
> First, make a list of everything you need, and how you believe that your content should be organized. Then, go out and start browsing both available themes as well as functioning websites in your industry to see what is working well.
>
> Don't fall in love with a beautiful theme that doesn't meet your needs. Keep looking for a perfect or near-perfect fit and then customize some elements if needed. "

Benjamine Morrison

WHAT'S A PLUGIN?

A plugin is an extra that you can add to your website to make it do something that it doesn't do "out of the box." For example, you could add a plugin to add an events calendar or an online store to your website. Plugins are usually made by independent developers who make them available to others (often at no charge). Whatever you want your website to do, there is usually a plugin that you can use. We mostly talk about plugins when talking about WordPress, however extras also exist for other platforms. You may see them referred to as Apps when you're using a system other than WordPress.

SELF-HOSTED WORDPRESS OR A HOSTED PLATFORM?

Self-hosted WordPress stands apart from all the other systems you can choose from because you are entirely in control of your website. You're not dependent on any other party staying in business, as you are if you sign up for a monthly contract with the platforms that provide you with hosting as well. This is a major advantage that for many users outweighs the fact that if you build your site with self-hosted WordPress, you are also responsible for technical hitches, security, etc. and you'll have to perform regular maintenance to keep your site in shape. As this is a free software, there's no "support" to rely on for help (although there is a vast community of other users who may voluntarily help you if you run into trouble).

You have a lot more options if you create your site with self-hosted WordPress: you can choose any theme, or add any plugin to your site. However, you have to take care of the technical side of things, and security is your own responsibility.

Far left: HTTP://WWW. THECREATIVEARTACADEMY.COM
Left: HTTPS://WWW. NICHARRY.COM

Because WordPress is so well known, people who want to get a website often assume that WordPress is the choice for them. But if you are building your website yourself, think carefully if you are up to the challenge of managing everything yourself; you may well find it easier to choose one of the "hosted" systems that take care of the techie side of things for you.

Over the last few years creating a site with self-hosted WordPress has become increasingly complicated. Templates offer more and more options; while the result is greater flexibility in what you can do with your WordPress website, it also means a steeper learning curve. If this isn't the kind of challenge you relish, this won't be the right choice for you.

WordPress.com vs. Self-hosted WordPress

WORDPRESS.COM

PROS

- It's great for blogs.
- Fast and easy to set up.
- You don't have to worry about technical problems.
- You don't have to worry about security.
- You have an instant network of readers.

CONS

- Limited range of themes.
- The premium themes cost more.
- You can't add plugins.
- If you ever want to get a programmer to tinker with the code of your site to change either the look of it or its functionality—you can't.
- You have limited storage space.
- You have to pay to prevent ads showing on your site (they don't often show up, but they can).
- If you ever want to run ads on your site, you're not allowed to.

SELF-HOSTED WORDPRESS

PROS

- You can use it to build any kind of site.
- You are independent.
- You can use whatever theme you like, even custom-designed ones.
- You can add plugins to make your site perform all kinds of functions.
- If you ever need to get a programmer to work on your site, you can.
- Your storage space is only limited by the hosting package you choose.
- A big community of other users.

CONS

- You have to install it yourself.
- Depending on your theme, setting up can be complicated.
- You have to take care of hosting.
- There's no centralized support to help you if you run into technical problems.
- You're in charge of security.
- You're in charge of backups.
- You need to do regular maintenance.

STRIKINGLY

HTTPS://WWW.STRIKINGLY.COM

Strikingly is an amazing innovation, probably the easiest way of getting yourself a website in existence at present; it allows you to create a simple, but very professional-looking one-page site with literally just a few clicks. One-page sites have become a trend over the last few years, and they're probably a trend that's here to stay—they're ideal for personal branding, but they can also work just as well for a more full-blown corporate website or to showcase a specific project.

A great way to start is to use their "One-Click" tool that creates a website from Facebook or LinkedIn within just seconds. From there, it's really easy to edit the pictures and wording and add and rearrange sections.

Strikingly's App Store allows you to stretch the functionality of the system, for example by adding a newsletter signup form, and more, and there are also built-in, simple, e-commerce and blogging features. Upgrading to a paid version allows you to use your own domain name, remove Strikingly branding, and add some more sophisticated layout tools such as a slider. Their templates are all mobile-friendly.

Strikingly is extremely easy to use but despite this, does have the potential to fulfill all your basic website needs, while looking polished and professional at the same time.

These two dynamic, attractive sites are great examples of what can be created using this very simple website builder.

Top: HTTP://WWW.WATERCRESSBALI.COM

Bottom: HTTP://WWW.LECOFFEEGUY.COM

EMILY PENN

STRIKINGLY

| UK | HTTP://WWW.EMILYPENN.CO.UK |

> I was looking for a platform that was really easy to edit and build myself, but would also look really beautiful on both computer and mobile device. I tried WordPress for a few years but I found it a bit clunky! Then I found Strikingly...

Strikingly makes lots of decisions for you, which is why it's so easy to use, but the decisions it makes for you are smart and beautiful so you end up with a stunning site without too much work.

The system has a very useful image editor but I like to be able to custom-make special tiles with words on them etc., to drop into my Strikingly site. I use Photoshop to do this.

My best advice is to keep it simple! It's so tempting to want to cram your site with everything possible, but the key is to figure out the most important bits and let them shine.

Less is more when it comes to text—work out how to distill what you want to say into as few words as possible and let the images do the talking.

Emily Penn

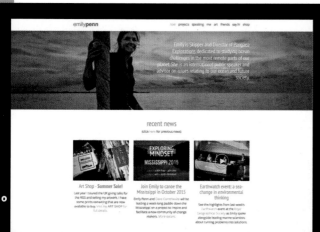

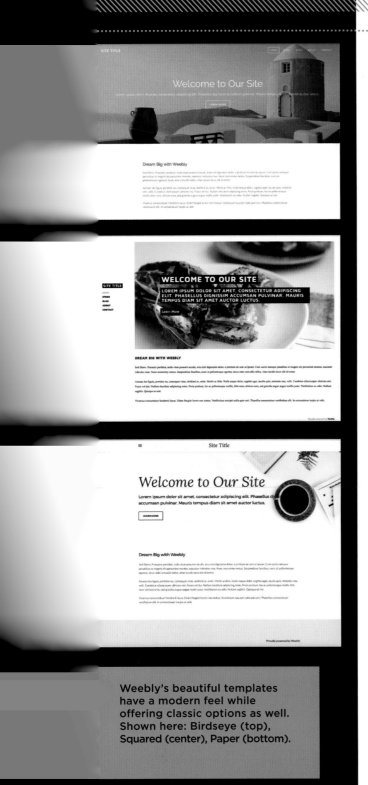

Weebly's beautiful templates have a modern feel while offering classic options as well. Shown here: Birdseye (top), Squared (center), Paper (bottom).

WEEBLY

HTTP://WWW.WEEBLY.COM

Weebly is vastly popular easy-to-use drag-and-drop website builder, and one of your best options if you want something that's supremely easy to use—it's arguably the very easiest to use of all the hosted website platforms if you want something that offers you more options than Strikingly does (such as several pages on the site).

There aren't as many templates to choose from as with Wix (see the next page), nor are the templates as flexible; but they do look great, and the suggested layouts for the different pages you're likely to need to create makes for a very professional-looking website with just a few clicks.

In addition, Weebly offers a built-in e-commerce feature, forum, survey tool, bookings system, to name but a few of the tools you can add to your site, and there are a good number of external add-ons if you need your site to "do" anything else. An added advantage is that if you do ever want to get a developer to work on your site, they will be able to access the code, and there is the facility to export your blog as well, supposing, for example, you wanted to switch to self-hosted WordPress a little further down the line.

In short, Weebly is an excellent option that you should certainly look into if you want a smooth and easy web-building experience, and want to avoid a learning curve!

SWELL MAGAZINE
WEEBLY

FRANCE | **HTTP://WWW.SWELLMAGAZINE.COM**

"**A**fter trying a few free WordPress themes and realizing I would need to hire someone to make my site even remotely resemble the sample WordPress sites, I gave up and instead followed the advice of a friend and chose Weebly. The WYSIWYG format really worked for me. I wanted simplicity and that's what I got.

The platform is ideal for someone like me who wanted to get something out there, with the idea of upgrading further down the line.

At the beginning, I was really worried about my website looking "empty" or amateurish due to lack of content. I don't have a huge catalog of writers and am still in the process of building the site, more than a year on. Surprisingly, this doesn't seem to deter people or affect the viewing experience in the ways I'd imagined it would. People who log onto Swell! frequently tell me that they think the site looks great, which is utterly surprising to me and my hyper-critical eye.

When browsing other sites, there's sometimes so much going on that the eye doesn't know where to focus. My sense is that people definitely expect new content, but also appreciate white space and a clean look, perhaps as a response to the overscheduled, busy lives we live. I think we crave simplicity and order in this chaos, and maybe clean website design offers a bit of that."

Aurelia d'Andrea

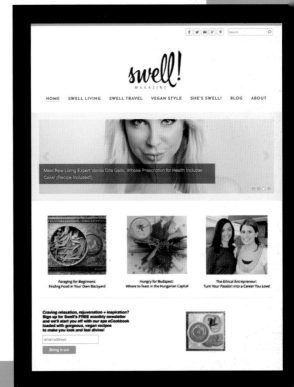

WIX

HTTP://WWW.WIX.COM

Wix is an alternative website-building platform, also very popular, that differs from Weebly in a few key ways. The platform allows you a large amount of flexibility; not only do they have a large selection of really great templates to choose from, specifically designed with for different fields of activity, but you can also create your own design entirely from scratch, if you want to, with a drag-and-drop interface. The tradeoff for this increased amount of flexibility is that it is a little more fiddly to use, but if you want to get creative, there'll be nothing stopping you.

There are a couple of drawbacks to using Wix, though, that you need to be aware of. One of these is the fact that you can't access the code of your website; at this stage, this mightn't be an issue, but in the future, you might potentially need to. In addition, you can't switch between templates without rebuilding the whole site, and you can't export your website content, which could be problematic if you end up creating a lot of content and then decide to move your site to another system.

However, Wix is a very good option if your project isn't vastly complicated or large-scale, and you want to be able to experiment with the design of your website.

As with Strikingly and Weebly, you have an array of "Apps" you can add to your site, and there's a built-in e-commerce feature as well.

FRENCH KNOT
WIX

| US | HTTP://WWW.FRENCHKNOTSTUDIOS.COM |

"Even the best web design can be horribly flawed by unprofessional pictures. Hire a photographer! The money is totally worth it in the long run. Share your web design with the photographer in advance so they can shoot with the proper orientation in mind, or know you're using a white background and want everything super light and airy, or a dark background and are looking for drama. The images, typefaces, graphics, etc., are all apart of the big picture, and should be carefully considered every step of the way.

Visit your competition's websites as well as those that are already a success. If you want to be a fashion designer, look as designers just starting out, but also look at Chanel. It's important to see what your direct competition is doing so you can identify their strengths and weaknesses and plan accordingly. See what you want to aspire to, and how they present themselves. Notice how they use their branding and incorporate some of those ideas into your project.

Make sure you get a comfy chair! Building a website is a marathon, not a sprint."

Audrey Wagner, photos by Izzy Hudgins

SQUARESPACE

HTTP://SQUARESPACE.COM

Squarespace is the slickest of all the hosted website builders, with a distinctively "designer" feel. This won't suit everyone, but if this fits your image, you may have found your perfect platform.

You can see that the Squarespace system has been designed with care, and this applies equally to how it actually works; everything fits together coherently and is intuitive to work with. The easy-to-use interface gives you complete control over how your pages are laid out: you make your changes while viewing what you're doing, which is much easier than working in a separate admin area, as you do with WordPress. Not only can you decide exactly what features to put where—text, images, contact form, newsletter signup, video, map, and so on, but you can easily customize every aspect of the look of your site, including fonts and colors. The platform includes an elegant blogging feature that is an integral part of your site, and all templates can incorporate e-commerce—although at the time of writing the only payment processor they accept is Stripe, which means in effect that e-commerce is only available to site owners in the US, UK, Canada, Ireland, and Australia. Do check this, though, as their reach is bound to extend in future.

Among many other benefits, users can access a library of Getty images, for which you pay a small fee each time you use a picture. You also get access to the whole range of Google fonts as well as Typekit fonts, and Squarespace has a built-in logo maker that gives you access to a vast library of icons. Their "cover page" facility allows for the quick and easy creation of one-page sites for personal branding, a specific product or event, or collecting email addresses.

Squarespace websites are, of course, entirely mobile-friendly.

Squarespace templates are stunning and are highly customizable, enabling you to create a site that looks both unique and very modern.
Top: HTTP://WWW.VICKI-TURNER.COM

Bottom: HTTP://WWW.MAI-HUDSON.ORG

SWEET GUM COMPANY

SQUARESPACE

US	HTTP://SWEETGUMCO.COM

"On my site, both the logo and the photos were professionally done. I think that the quality of the photography in particular is critical for making the site look professional.

Given that the internet is an entirely visual medium, ensuring the quality of the visual is of the utmost importance.

I'm very pleased with Squarespace. They have great layout options and their controls are fairly intuitive. They also have extensive online information sections, and I've received prompt personal help when I've needed to actually interact with someone."

Joseph Huebscher, originally created by Elizabeth Evelyn Kirby

OTHER *hosted website* BUILDERS

WEBS, JIMDO, & YOLA

Webs, Jimdo, and Yola are three popular hosted platforms that have been around for a while, all of them very user-friendly. You'd be able to get a goodlooking, functional website with any of these. Even though my personal preference at the time of writing would be one of the hosted systems talked about over the previous pages, updates and innovations do occur often, so it will be worth your while checking these established platforms out for yourself.

HTTP://WWW.WEBS.COM
HTTP://WWW.JIMDO.COM
HTTPS://WWW.YOLA.COM

THE GRID

Right at the other end of the scale in terms of modernity, The Grid is a cutting-edge, long awaited, much-heralded automatic website maker that uses artificial intelligence to create unique websites from your photos, videos, written content, and social feeds; at the time of writing, the system is in pre-launch, but it's one to watch out for.

HTTPS://THEGRID.IO/

If you're a musician, a photographer, or a creative who needs to display your portfolio online, take a look at the following platforms designed especially for your specific needs.

FOR MUSICIANS

Website builders, selling music online and digital distribution:

HTTPS://BANDZOOGLE.COM
HTTPS://WWW.REVERBNATION.COM
HTTPS://BANDCAMP.COM

FOR PHOTOGRAPHERS

Sites, storage, selling prints online:

HTTPS://WWW.SMUGMUG.COM—store photos and create websites, with built-in online store for professionals.
HTTP://WWW.PHOTOSHELTER.COM
HTTPS://22SLIDES.COM
HTTPS://EXPOSURE.CO—for "photo stories" rather than full-blown websites.

FOR CREATIVES

Hosted online portfolio makers:

HTTP://DUNKED.COM
HTTP://FORMAT.COM
HTTPS://CARBONMADE.COM

WE ALL NEED TO CALM DOWN

BANDZOOGLE

FRANCE | **HTTP://WEALLNEEDTOCALMDOWN.COM**

"My main challenge in building We All Need To Calm Down was trusting my own abilities and getting over my belief that I couldn't build a beautiful site without outside help. I've had many music websites in my career, all of them were built for me by talented designers, so it was daunting at first to try it myself. Once I accepted that I would spend a lot of time doing trial and errors, it became easier.

I find photos are the easiest way to convey a visual feeling on a website. I had my photos chosen first and I really built the site around the. It really helped speed up the process and focus the look of the site immediately. I scoured photo essay books and font websites for ideas and inspiration—it was helpful for me to know going in what I like and don't like.

I could not be happier with Bandzoogle. I love the fact that it is made specifically for musicians, is extremely user friendly, and they offer a wide variety of templates to choose from. All templates can also be customized. Their customer service is impeccable as well, very quick and extremely responsive. I would definitely recommend this platform to any musician. "

Dana Boulé

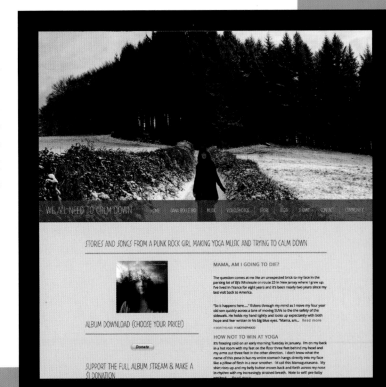

BLOGGING *platforms*

If you want to set up a blog as an addition to your main website, rather than creating a blog in its own right, it makes sense to have your blog integrated into your website, as this looks smarter. Because blogging is so important, most of the website-building platforms today offer a built-in blog element. If blogging is going to be a major activity, you will want to be sure it has all the features you'll need and isn't too basic; WordPress (both versions) and Squarespace are the most sophisticated blogging systems and it may make sense to opt for one of these.

It's also possible to "bolt on" an external blog to your main website, so don't worry if you have an existing, thriving blog on WordPress .com, for example, and you're about to create a new website using Wix—you can connect the two. The most polished way of doing this is to create a subdomain, which appears as (for example) "blog.mydomain.com"; you then add the subdomain to your site menu, labeled "Blog." (How you create a subdomain and point it to your blog depends on your domain name registrar and the platform you are using; you will find instructions as to how to do this in the "help" section of your platform's website.)

BLOGGING OPTIONS

Whether you choose the self-hosted version or the hosted one, WordPress is the obvious system to use when you're setting up a blog, but the free, Google-owned Blogger (BlogSpot) network has many devotees as well (https://www.blogger.com). It's much less customizable and doesn't look as professional, but it could be that simplicity, with no extra costs, is what you're looking for.

There are other good blogging options around, too. Among these are Ghost (https://ghost.org)—a beautiful, clean-looking new setup for blogs—and Posthaven (https://posthaven.com). Medium (https://medium.com) is a relatively new and popular option, however it differs from the others in that very little customization is possible; the main attraction being the instant readership—so it's more of a way of getting your articles read on the web, rather than creating any kind of online identity of your own.

◁ Julia Kodl's art website links to an external blog (and her Etsy shop).
HTTP://WWW.JULIAKODLART.COM

EXPERT VAGABOND
SELF-HOSTED WORDPRESS

| USA | HTTP://EXPERTVAGABOND.COM |

> Spend a little money on a professional theme. A good design is a wonderful marketing tool that doesn't cost much. First impressions are everything!

For the past five years I've maintained and customized my own WordPress site. Luckily there is a wealth of knowledge about the platform out there, so when I encounter a problem (database crash, plugin conflicts, etc.) I can usually find the solution with a Google search.

The best thing about my blogging, travelling lifestyle is that I'm self-employed and location independent, so I'm free to just take off and travel anywhere at anytime. The biggest challenge is to build up the self-discipline to slow down, stay put, and get work done. It's easy to procrastinate when there are no immediate repercussions, and take the day off and head to the beach rather than working.

Make sure you stick with blogging for the long-term. Some people may get lucky, but most of us worked at it for years before we were able to earn a living from it. It's a never-ending learning process. **"**

Matthew Karsten

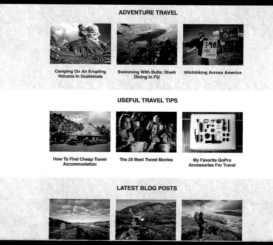

SHOPIFY

HTTPS://WWW.SHOPIFY.COM

We've seen that many hosted website builders also incorporate an e-commerce system, of greater or lesser complexity. If your site is primarily a webstore, you may wish to consider a platform that is designed specifically for online stores. This will have an impact in terms of layout; templates designed specifically as webstores will offer better ways of showing off your products—sliders, featured products, best sellers, etc.—as well as offering you features that will be important in the running of your business: integrations with fulfillment houses, stock control, special offers, coupon codes, mailing list integration, and so on.

The best webstore option, as I see it, for DIY website builders, is Shopify. It wins hands-down over other webstore systems in that it is designed in such a way that the business owner really can set up the shop, from scratch, without a developer. Other systems are difficult to configure and can't be customized without going into the code—that's not to say you can't use a developer for your Shopify store if you want to, but you really can do everything you need to do by yourself, with no difficulty.

Obviously a cutting-edge company like Shopify has responsive themes; they also offer a mobile-friendly admin view so that you can manage your store and your orders directly from your smartphone. The checkout comes in more than 50 languages and there are over a hundred beautiful, easily configurable themes—these all have variations so there are in fact even more.

Just as impressive as the fantastic array of beautiful designs is the range of integrations available with Shopify. You can sync with third-party marketing, social media, order fulfillment, customer service, and accounting tools so that your webstore is streamlined with the way you run your business; they can also provide you with a point-of-sale card reader that allows you to take payment via your webstore in person.

At the time of writing, Shopify can work with over 70 global payment processors, plus their own Shopify payments system, which is fully integrated with their admin are , and helps you cut down on transaction costs. This isn't available worldwide at present, but do check on this; Shopify is a very popular and fast-moving platform that is being developed all the time.

THE SHOPIFY BUY BUTTON

A feature that may be useful for some is a simple "Buy" button that means you can sell items from your website via Shopify, without having the full webstore setup.

SELL ON PINTEREST

Shopify also allows you to add a "Buy" button to your Pinterest pins, which means that people can buy without having to leave Pinterest! This is called a "Buyable Pin."

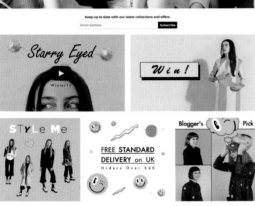

Left: Setting up your webstore with Shopify is a brilliant way of getting a striking, modern, professional-looking website. Great photos and graphics, such as those seen here, help too.

HTTP://WWW.THEWHITEPEPPER.COM

Below: Shopify's themes are stunning to look at and very easy to configure. Seen here (from below left): Canopy (Kiln), Solo (Sepia), Retina (Amsterdam), and Masonry (Chameleon).

BIG CARTEL

HTTPS://WWW.BIGCARTEL.COM

Big Cartel is a nice, easy webstore platform that has none of the flashiness of Shopify but nonetheless does the job well for its users. It's aimed at the arts and crafts market, not for any kind of large-scale production, and works very well either as a stand-alone webstore or as an add-on to a main website or a blog.

There aren't that many themes, but the admin area allows you to customize many items; background, colors, and fonts. This means the webstore can be attached unobtrusively to any other website (you'll probably want to use a subdomain) and can be customized to fit in with the look. Big Cartel doesn't have many options, and is restricted to two payment processors (PayPal and Stripe), but the lack of "extras" means it does what it's meant to do, simply and well, and meets its target market's needs, without being a huge undertaking to set up.

SUPADUPA

SupaDupa's another option you may want to look at if you've been selling on Etsy or another craft marketplace and you're ready to upgrade to your own webstore, but don't want anything too complex. Their templates can be customized with colors and fonts; a particular benefit is that you can import from a selection of other platforms including Etsy, ArtFire or Zibbet.

HTTP://SUPADUPA.ME

Big Cartel caters for the artist or small-scale creator.
HTTPS://WWW.BIGCARTEL.COM

Leah Goren's store is an add-c her main site; Big Cartel's clea unobtrusive themes, with easi changeable fonts and colors, be made to work with any distinctive "look."
HTTP://SHOP.LEAHGOREN.COM

E-commerce with WORDPRESS

Another way of creating a full-on, professional-looking webstore is via self-hosted WordPress. To do this, you'll need an e-commerce plugin, plus a specially-designed e-commerce theme to go with it. There are several plugins to choose from; WooCommerce is at the moment the most popular and as a result, pretty much all the WordPress themes designed as online stores are set up to work with it. You may also see themes that are created for for WP eCommerce and Jigoshop—these are two other well-known e-commerce plugins, but the one we'll look at in this book is WooCommerce.

Installing WooCommerce is free and you can do this from the admin area of your WordPress site; you don't have to download it first. There are loads of different paid-for add-ons

("extensions") available that work with WooCommerce: memberships, subscriptions, invoices, product add-ons to allow for customization, SagePay integration, product labels, etc. WooCommerce can work with dozens of different global payment processors.

In theory, configuring WooCommerce should be within the comfort zone of a first-time DIY website builder—we'll see how it's done in Chapter 4—but do note that if you add extensions, they need to be updated yearly, and any complex requirements might be too complex to configure. If what you want to do means you have to install add-ons, you might be better off with a non-WordPress solution such as Shopify, which will remove the technical side of things from the equation.

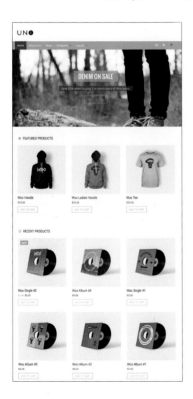

◁ WooCommerce was developed by WooThemes. They have a good selection of beautiful-looking e-commerce themes designed to run with their plugin, however most e-commerce themes designed by independent developers also work with WooCommerce, so you are not limited to themes created by WooThemes (http://www.woothemes .com). Shown here, Uno theme by WooThemes (far left), and the Shop page of Jasmine theme by Angie Makes (http://angiemakes. com, left). You can choose to show the store on the front page, or not.

Other options for SELLING ONLINE

We've seen a number of platforms that are designed specifically as online stores. But you're not limited to these. If you already have an existing site and you just want to add e-commerce, one of the following options might be just the thing for you.

△ **Gumroad is a popular system for taking payment online.**
HTTPS://GUMROAD.COM

△ **You can add an online store with Ecwid, whatever platform you use.**
HTTP://WWW.ECWID.COM

△ **Spaces lets you get your products on sale with just a few clicks.**
HTTPS://GOSPACES.COM

GUMROAD

Gumroad is a brilliantly easy way of selling online. You simply direct purchasers to your Gumroad page with a website link (or set up a widget), and Gumroad send you payment from your sales every other Friday, directly into your bank account if you're US-based, or via PayPal (at the time of writing) if you're anywhere else. They can also take pre-orders and subscription payments, as well as handle the VAT issue for global sale of digital goods (we talk about this in Chapter 14).

ECWID

Ecwid is entirely different kind of solution. It's an easy-to-implement, cross-platform shopping cart system that you can simply plug into any type of website using one of a range of global payment processors. An added plus is that with the app you can use Ecwid as a mobile point of sale, and it can also integrate with Facebook or Tumblr; you can, in effect, can have a store without having a site at all.

SPACES

Spaces is the simplest way of setting up a sales website that you could imagine—it creates one-page sites, to which you can add pictures, text, products, or a signup form. That's it!

Online MARKETPLACES

If you prefer not to get into the details of selling from your own website. There are plenty of online marketplaces you can use instead—this is a much easier way of selling, without the responsibility of taking payment yourself, plus you also get the benefit of "passing traffic." The best-known of all these marketplaces is Etsy, but there are many other places you can go to as well to show your products to a crowd of people ready and waiting to buy them.

△ Etsy is the obvious, and best-known, place for crafters and artisans to sell their wares.
HTTPS://WWW.ETSY.COM

△ A new, innovative marketplace that puts emphasis on the individuality of each artist.
HTTPS://WWW.ZIIBRA.COM

△ A popular alternative to Etsy that has taken off over the last few years.
HTTPS://WWW.ZIBBET.COM

△ A marketplace for "indie brands"; individual sellers are encouraged to build their own brand.
HTTP://WWW.STORENVY.COM

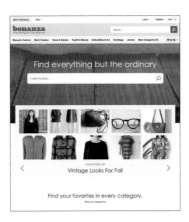

△ Bonanza was voted the best marketplace for sellers, by sellers, for four consecutive years.
HTTP://WWW.BONANZA.COM

△ Handmade at Amazon:
HTTP://SERVICES.AMAZON.COM/ HANDMADE/HANDMADE.HTM

3 Planning *Your Website*

RESEARCHING *your* WEBSITE

The best way to work out how you want your website to look, and what content you want it to include, is to look at other websites. If you're an actor, look at other actors' websites; if you're a writer, look at other writers'; or life coaches', or photographers'—etc. Look at the sites of people at the same level as you, to get an idea of what the "competition" is doing, as well as those at the top of your field, to think about where you may be aiming.

Consider carefully how their sites look, how they structure their information, and what content and other elements they include. Jot down notes with a pen and paper or a word processor; screenshots are also extremely useful as an aide-mémoire (see the tip box on page 56).

After surfing around for a while, you'll be able to see what your peers are doing that you also want to do, and with any luck you'll also have come up with some ideas of things that they are not doing that you can implement to make your site stand out from theirs. With this information, make a list of the pages you'll need on your site, and the elements that you want to include on those pages. The next pages and the features checklist on page 69 will help you.

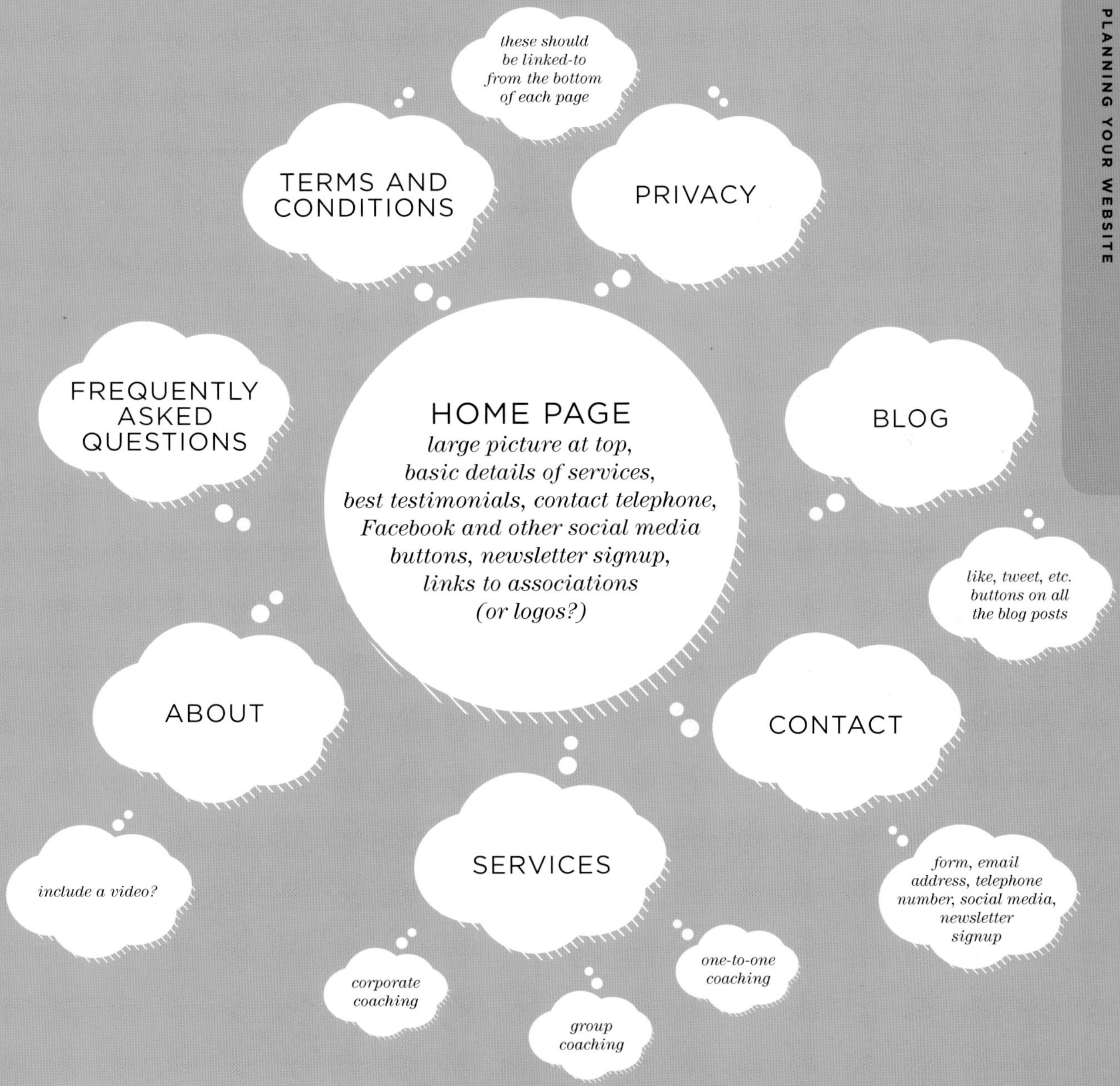

*these should
be linked-to
from the bottom
of each page*

TERMS AND
CONDITIONS

PRIVACY

FREQUENTLY
ASKED
QUESTIONS

HOME PAGE
*large picture at top,
basic details of services,
best testimonials, contact telephone,
Facebook and other social media
buttons, newsletter signup,
links to associations
(or logos?)*

BLOG

*like, tweet, etc.
buttons on all
the blog posts*

ABOUT

CONTACT

include a video?

SERVICES

*form, email
address, telephone
number, social media,
newsletter
signup*

*corporate
coaching*

*one-to-one
coaching*

*group
coaching*

Supposing you were setting
up a site for your life-coaching
practice, your list of pages and
functions to include might look
something like this.

TAKING SCREENSHOTS

To take a screenshot on a PC, press the PrtScn button, navigate to Word (or any other suitable application) and paste in the copied content (shortcut Ctrl+V). To take a screenshot on a Mac, press Command-Shift-4, then use your mouse to draw a rectangle around the content you want to copy; paste the copied content into your Word (or other) document (Cmd+V).

TARGETING YOUR WEBSITE TO YOUR IDEAL SITE VISITORS

Who is your target audience? Before you start designing and before you start writing your website content, you need to be clear on this. Your ideal site visitors are either your potential customers, or, if you're not actually selling anything from your site, the people for whom you are creating it—whether you're showcasing your acting skills in order to be hired, or your writing, or other professional skills. Make sure you speak the language your target audience speaks; show you understand their needs and are in their world.

Your site needs to resonate with your customers, rather than your colleagues or other people in the same field as you. For example, if you decide to set up a blog on your accountancy website, for all the excellent reasons that we'll talk about in Chapter 8, you won't want to be writing industry-specific articles that will only interest other accountants, but you'll want to talk to your potential clients about useful, basic information that's suitable and interesting for non-accountants.

WHAT MAKES A GOOD WEBSITE?

You most likely visit dozens of websites a day and know instinctively which ones you like and which you don't like. But it's now time to get a little bit more analytical and think why some websites work and others don't.

Here are some factors to consider:
- Appearance—does it convey the right impression? Is the "look" right for the website's visitors?
- Tone—does the website connect with its visitors? Does it signal that it is on the same wavelength by using the language that they use?
- Is it easy to read? Plenty of white space is always a good thing, together with good, clear layout of text.
- Clarity—is it clear what the website is about, and what its owner is offering?
- Is it easy to understand the layout and find what you are looking for?
- Is the site up to date?
- Is it interesting and engaging enough for you to want to return, or sign up to a newsletter to make sure you keep in touch?

Most importantly, from the website owner's perspective:
- Does the website fulfill the purpose for which it was created?

BE ORIGINAL

Researching other sites is the best way of getting ideas, but this doesn't mean copying—it's important that your site resonates as genuine, and aside from it being unethical to copy, you don't want to look like a mere imitation of someone more established or experienced than you.

SARAH + ABRAHAM

SHOPIFY

| USA | HTTP://WWW.SARAHANDABRAHAM.COM |

"When I started my business in 2007 I contacted a website developer, and she advised me to start out with an Etsy shop before launching my own website. I didn't like that advice at the time, but it was absolutely the best thing I could have done.

I received a ton of feedback from Etsy shoppers and ended up building an entirely new product line based on that. By the time I commissioned my first website a year later I had a much better understanding of what my target customers were looking for and willing to pay for.

Shopify is extremely user friendly. I'm easily able to add and update categories and products. ShipStation has been a huge time saver for me. It makes shipping super easy. I was initially hesitant to sign up for an app with a monthly fee, but it's worth every penny."

Sara Tams

ORGANIZING *your* *website* CONTENT

Web designers use something called a "wireframe" to work out a website's layout. This is a sketch of what's going to be shown on each page, how the layout is going to work, and how the site will function. You don't need to create anything so detailed for the pages on your site because you will probably be using a ready-made template that will determine, to some extent, your basic layout*. Making a sketch of the hierarchy of your site, and what will be included on each page will keep you clear on your purpose, clarify the menu structure, and make it easier to choose the right template.

For our example life coach's website, we can see that it's a good idea to group the different services offered into a "drop-down" menu in order to save space and keep things clear (see opposite), and we can see that there is a need for quite a few different elements on the home page. Working this out now will help you choose a suitable template for the website at the next stage.

* Wix does allow you to create your design without using a template, but most readers will be working with a pre-defined layout.

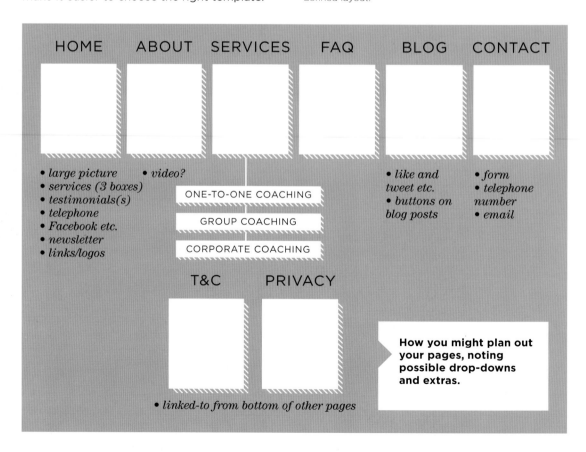

HOME   ABOUT   SERVICES   FAQ   BLOG   CONTACT

- *large picture*
- *services (3 boxes)*
- *testimonials(s)*
- *telephone*
- *Facebook etc.*
- *newsletter*
- *links/logos*

- *video?*

ONE-TO-ONE COACHING

GROUP COACHING

CORPORATE COACHING

- *like and tweet etc.*
- *buttons on blog posts*

- *form*
- *telephone number*
- *email*

T&C   PRIVACY

- *linked-to from bottom of other pages*

How you might plan out your pages, noting possible drop-downs and extras.

| HOME | ABOUT | ▾ SERVICES | FAQ | BLOG | CONTACT |

▸ ONE-TO-ONE COACHING
▸ GROUP COACHING
▸ CORPORATE COACHING

◁ A drop-down menu helps save space—the different categories of coaching only appear when the user passes their mouse over "Services." Note that we have chosen to put "FAQ" in the menu instead of "Frequently Asked Questions," in order to save even more space.

PLANNING YOUR MENU

Your menu—otherwise known as your navigation—is how your visitors find their way around your site.

Avoid a cluttered menu, or one that wraps (meaning that it takes two lines instead of just one—this can look messy). If you have many pages that you need to include in the main menu, use a "drop-down" system to keep the navigation clean and tidy.

Your main menu should remain the same throughout the site. (If your site is large, there is nothing stopping you including additional menu items somewhere else, for example in a column to the side, just make sure you keep the main menu as clean as possible.)

525 STUDIO
STRIKINGLY

| SINGAPORE | HTTP://WWW.525STUDIO.COM |

"Your website is a representation of you as a company or as a person. So make a good first impression. The main challenges of setting up our website were the research and the trial and error that went into it. We took a couple of months looking at some really creative website layouts—our website had to be on-trend and at the same time communicate to our potential clients at one glance what our company is all about. My advice is less is always more. Cut out the unnecessary and show more of what is important. "

Iman Jaya

The PAGES on your WEBSITE

The pages you need on your site will obviously depend on the kind of site you are creating. Every site needs a Home page, an About page, and a Contact page. Beyond this—products, services, portfolio, testimonials pages, shop, and so on—depends on your individual project.

THE HOME PAGE

Your Home page is the first page people see. You often have just a few seconds to show the site visitor that they have come to the right site for what they are looking for, or impress them—what you want to achieve when people arrive on your site depends on what your aim is—but the crucial point is that this information, or the right impression, has to be conveyed instantaneously.

With this in mind, think what you want to show at first glance: a striking image to draw the visitor in? Your press credentials, your best-selling products, your best testimonials, or your latest blog posts? If you're collecting emails for an email mailing list (which we'll discuss in Chapter 10), you'll certainly want the signup form to be near the top of the page.

Long page layouts with one element following after another are increasingly in use as they're practical for mobile viewing. If your site is going to work like this, make sure the most important elements are right up at the top.

△ Sarah Jenks's "Live More Weigh Less" website invites visitors to watch an introductory video as soon as they arrive on the website; her email signup is right underneath it, together with press logos in a highly visible position.

HTTPS://SARAHJENKS.COM
Design: home page krissdidit.com, branding/internal pages janereaction.com

THE "ABOUT" PAGE

The "About" page on a website is generally
the most-viewed after the home page, so you
need to consider very carefully the text that
you put here. Oddly, this is the page that is
the most often neglected by website owners,
perhaps because they find it embarrassing
to talk about themselves. But it's the perfect
opportunity to present yourself or your
business and engage your site visitors. When
you're crafting the content for your "About"
page, consider the following:

- Do you want to sound more formal, or
  more friendly? Using the third person
  can sometimes sound stand-offish.
- Using jargon is always alienating—avoid it.
- Buzzwords or clichés that don't really
  mean anything aren't useful—can you
  provide facts and figures instead? (For
  example, avoid a phrase like "top-of-the-
  range customer service" and instead say
  something like "We always respond to our
  customers' enquiries within less than 24
  hours, even at the weekends.")
- Including some "human" information helps
  your visitors to get a better picture of you—
  this works even if your site is a serious
  business website; in fact it could be even
  more important.
- Telling the story behind your business is a
  really good way of bringing it to life and
  making it memorable for the site visitor.

Your aim is to make yourself, or your business,
stand out and resonate.

△ Giving the backstory to a company, including a
profile of each person involved, brings a website
to life—this is a brilliant example.
HTTP://GROVEMADE.COM

THE "CONTACT" PAGE

Your "Contact" page needs to provide as many ways of contacting you as possible. As well as a web form, it's important that you also include an email address so that people can email you directly rather than using the form (some people are suspicious of using web forms, and others like to have a record of your email address in their "Sent" box). Don't consider your email address a secret—people need it to contact you. It should be spam-protected (sometimes this is automatic; refer to your platform to check) and it should be "live"—that means that an email should open up directly when it's clicked on.

If possible, give a telephone number so that people can contact you by telephone (many people prefer to pick up the phone), and if you're a brick-and-mortar business, give your address, opening hours, transport and parking details, and consider including a Google map as well. Your contact page can also include your social media profiles and a newsletter signup form.

Make it easy for people to contact you—include a link to your "Contact" page in your main menu (it's usually the last item). Don't make people search for it hidden somewhere else on your site.

NAMING YOUR PAGES

How you name your pages will depend on whether your site is classic or more original. For a conventional business site you'll most likely want to stick with the obvious ways of naming pages: "Services," "Projects," etc. For a more creative, original site, you may want to dream up some quirkier or more striking page titles. Consider the balance between being original and being clear; site visitors need to be able to understand quickly what information is to be found on which page on your site, so steer away from anything obscure.

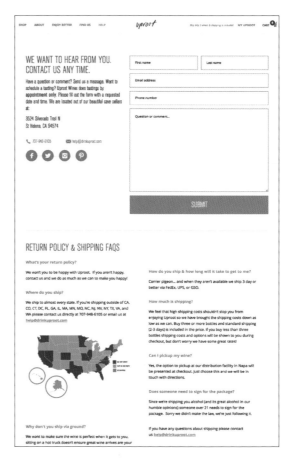

▷ Entrepreneurial wine company Uproot has the perfect example of a contact page. As well as a form to make contacting them easy, they provide a visible, clickable email address, telephone number, real world address, and social media buttons. They also include their return policy and FAQs on this page, and their contact details are clearly shown at the bottom of every page.
HTTP://WWW.DRINKUPROOT.COM

PAGE CHECKLIST

WHICH OF THESE DO YOU NEED ON YOUR SITE?

○ *Home*

○ *About*

○ *Services*

○ *Portfolio*

○ *Gallery*

○ *Videos*

○ *Clients*

○ *Testimonials*

○ *Pricing*

○ *Frequently Asked Questions*

○ *How to Find Us*

○ *Shop*

○ *Team*

○ *Blog*

○ *Awards*

○ *Publications*

○ *Press*

○ *Events*

○ *Filmography/ Discography*

○ *Lookbook*

○ *Feedback*

○ *Biography*

○ *Terms and Conditions*

○ *Returns*

○ *Privacy**

○ *Cookies**

○ *Contact*

*See chapter 14.

PREPARING *your* TEXT

When you've established what pages you need on the site and how they're going to be organized, you can prepare the text for your site. There are people who prefer to write directly into the pages as they create the site, but most find it easier to type into Word or into another text editor (it's less distracting, plus you have the advantage of a spell checker). You can then copy and paste the content into your actual site pages*.

*Some platforms (such as Squarespace) may copy across unwanted formatting from Word. For this reason, you should use their "Paste as Plain Text" tool (you'll see this button when you're inside their text editing area).

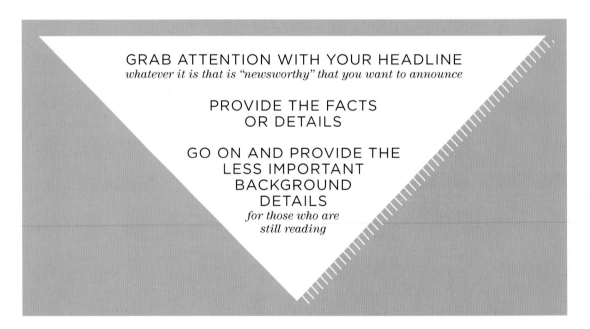

GRAB ATTENTION WITH YOUR HEADLINE
whatever it is that is "newsworthy" that you want to announce

PROVIDE THE FACTS
OR DETAILS

GO ON AND PROVIDE THE
LESS IMPORTANT
BACKGROUND
DETAILS
*for those who are
still reading*

WRITING FOR THE WEB

Writing for the web isn't the same as writing for print. With the internet, people expect to find the information they are looking for right away, so you need to cut out wordy waffle. That's not to say you need to be dry—on the contrary, you can put in as much personality as you like, but you need to keep your sentences short, be as engaging as possible, and break your content up into very short paragraphs or lists.

Plenty of white space makes it easier on the visitor's eye, as well as making it easier to scan for the essential information; make maximum use of headings, subheadings, numbered lists, and bullets, again to ensure optimum readability. Break up text-heavy pages by adding visuals— find suitable photos to add to the pages (see Chapter 6), or consider diagrams instead.

When you're writing, think about the journalists' inverted pyramid style of presenting material. Present the most

CALLS TO ACTION

Include what are known in marketing speak as "calls to action"—simple instructions to the site visitor to encourage them into an interaction with you—the end result of which is that they become a client, sign up for your newsletter, or follow your blog.

▽ The clear calls to action on this virtual assistant website take the visitor to the website's "Contact" page.
HTTP:// WWW.THEVIRTUALLYCONNECTED.COM

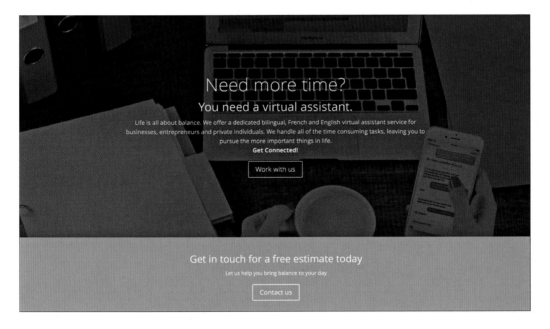

important "newsworthy" facts right up at the top (which is also good for search engine ratings). Then give the essential information, and only beneath that give the background material. (Normally we'd give the background information first to set the scene, then build up to what actually happened; this journalistic technique is sometimes called "frontloading"). Don't get too hung up on this—but it is a very useful way of presenting information when you're working out how to get across what you need to on the pages of your website.

YOUR TEXT AND THE SEARCH ENGINES

The text that you put on the pages of your website has an important impact on how your site is ranked in the search engines, so it makes sense to read Chapter 11 before you start writing.

Putting your VISITORS FIRST

If you're selling from your website, whether it's a service or products from an online store—or even if you're encouraging your visitors to sign up to your newsletter—write your text so that you put your visitors' needs first. This means that you need to stress the benefits they will receive rather than the features your products or your services (or your newsletters) offer.

For example, suppose you're listing some of the features your virtual assistant service offers its clients:

- **Clients only pay for the hours worked.**
- **We can deal with a wide range of tasks, even small ones.**
- **7-day-a-week service.**

These features are valuable ones but they can each be turned around so that the benefits to the customer are spelled out more obviously:

- **Peace of mind—we only bill you for the hours we've worked, to ensure you don't pay more than you need.**
- **Keep feelings of overwhelm at bay—we can help you with anything; no task is too small.**
- **Get support at all times—you can reach one of our staff every day, even at the weekends.**

This is one of the most important rules of copywriting and it's worth devoting attention to, to make sure your website copy is as effective as it can be.

Of course, the idea of putting your visitors first doesn't just apply to the way you write your text—as we have seen, you need to make your site easily navigable so they can find what they want with no problems, and, of course, the entire "look" of the site, from the template you choose to the graphics you display, needs to resonate with your target audience.

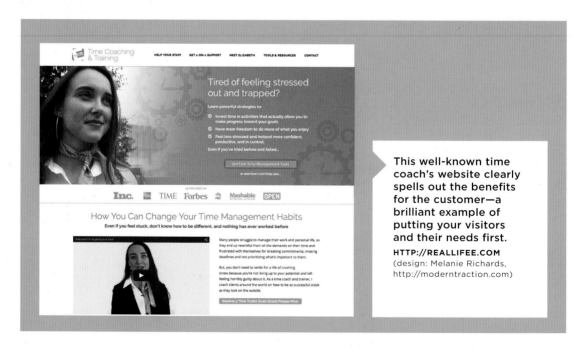

This well-known time coach's website clearly spells out the benefits for the customer—a brilliant example of putting your visitors and their needs first.
HTTP://REALLIFEE.COM
(design: Melanie Richards, http://moderntraction.com)

INKED DESIGNS
SELF-HOSTED WORDPRESS

USA	HTTP://WWW.THINKINKEDDESIGNS.COM

> "Your site is the representation of yourself to future clients. Put your best foot forward. But I would also say don't be afraid to show a bit of your personality. Design with your client in mind. Put yourself in their shoes. What do you want them to see first, second, last? If you were looking for the same product/service you are offering, what would you want to see on their site—what would make you buy from them?

White space is your friend. Don't try to fill every corner of your site with content. I would rather have clean empty white space than a site that is too busy or cluttered. Before you make your site live, let a friend or two go on the site to make sure it is aesthetically pleasing, user friendly, easy to navigate, etc.—test it on different browsers as well.

I did a lot of research and watched a bunch of tutorials before I started but it was a lot easier than I anticipated. It took me about a week from start to finish to make the site. I like how WordPress lets you to use plugins, which allows you to customize your site and add features that don't necessarily come with the template. It allows you to add a personal touch to your site."

Elayna Speight

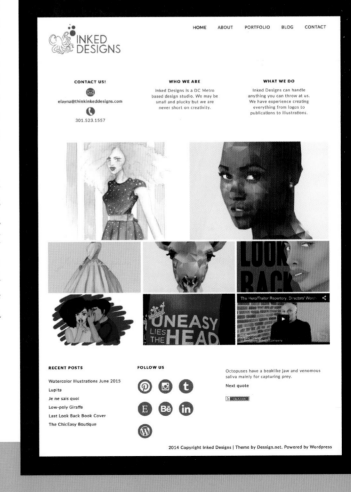

Establishing TRUST

A website needs to try to establish a feeling of trust between the website owner(s) and the site visitor in a way that we wouldn't need to do if we were actually connecting in a real-world environment. Your site visitors don't know you when they arrive on your website—so how can you replace the welcoming smile, the handshake, the reassuring interaction of a real-world encounter, on your website?

There are several things you can do to create a feeling that you are a real, trustworthy person running a real, trustworthy business (or whatever it is that you do). Here are some of them:

- Make sure your site looks professional. This doesn't mean dry or lacking personality—on the contrary, personality is important. But you must look as though you mean business and this means attending to broken links promptly and checking your website regularly for errors.
- Include client testimonials, with names and photos of the clients, if appropriate.
- Include real background information about you as a human, and potentially your staff as well—as we discussed on page 61 when we looked at "About" pages.
- Include photographs of the office, the studio, the workplace, you (and the staff) at work.
- Spell out your cast-iron guarantees.
- Be completely transparent about any potentially hidden costs (e.g. shipping abroad, etc.).
- Specify your return terms (which should be generous) and if applicable, provide tracking details for deliveries.
- Address potential queries or obstacles to purchase or engagement on your FAQ page.
- Respond to enquiries as fast as you possibly can.
- Include client logos if relevant.
- Include press or association logos, again if relevant.
- If you're selling online, display payment system logos.
- Social media "likes" and "follows" act as a public measure of peer approval*. If you have a good number of these, display the numbers; if not, don't show them, for the time being.
- Displaying telephone numbers and a real-world address is very useful for establishing trust. But as online-only setups get more and more common, it's increasingly acceptable not to include a physical address, as long as your other credentials show you're bona fide.
- Make sure your site is up to date. If it isn't, it looks as though you've disappeared, or gone under.

*See Chapter 10.

FEATURES CHECKLIST

○ *Contact form*

○ *Newsletter signup**

○ *Social media buttons linking to the profile pages***

○ *Social media "like" or "follow" buttons right within the website*

○ *Social media "share" buttons*

○ *Twitter feed*

○ *Photostreams (Instagram or Flickr)*

○ *Videos*

○ *Audio*

○ *Map*

○ *Blog*

○ *Subscribe to blog*

○ *Bookings*

○ *Calendar*

○ *Events*

○ *Online store (or simple PayPal payment buttons)*

○ *Photo gallery*

○ *Slideshow*

○ *Rotating image slider*

○ *Call to action bar****

○ *Client, press or association logos*

○ *Payment system logos*

○ *Book or ebook links (Amazon, B&N, Kindle, Nook)*

* See Chapter 9
** See Chapter 10
*** See page 161

4 Getting *Set Up*

Starting off with your CHOSEN PLATFORM

This chapter will show you the basic setup process for some of the most popular platforms, and give you a basic tour around how the admin area works. Some of the platforms are so easy to use that you'll find yourself moving around the admin area more or less intuitively in a short time, but others are a little more complex, notably self-hosted WordPress, for which you'll need more precise instructions, seeing as you need to install it on your hosting before you get started.

We'll also look at how to install WooCommerce —currently the most popular e-commerce plugin for WordPress—for those who want to use WordPress to build an online store.

Setting up WORDPRESS.COM

1. Click the blue "Create Website" button on the WordPress.com home page.

2. Choose any theme just to get started. You'll obviously take some time to choose the theme you really want to use, but this you can easily do once you're set up.

3. The next step offers you to purchase a domain, or connect a domain you already own to WordPress.com, but you may not be ready to do this yet. If that's the case, you'll want to use the free option for the time being. Choose the name for your website that will be in use until you attach a domain, and type it into the field (your free website address will be: "yourchoice. wordpress.com"). Don't be surprised if you have to try several times to find a name that hasn't been taken—thousands of people use WordPress.com! When you find the name you want, click the "Select" button next to the "Free" option.

4. At the next stage, choose the "Free for life" option—you can upgrade to one of the paid-for plans, if you want to, later.

5. Type in your email address, desired username and password.

6. Check your email and click the confirmation link in the email.

7. You'll be taken to a page with several options to help you get started. The one at the top is labeled "Customize Your Site," and while this might seem the most obvious first step, the first thing you'll really need to do is choose the best theme for you, and after you've chosen it, you can set about customizing it. So click instead on the "Select a Theme" button. Now, spend some time looking at themes; the one at the top left is the one that is currently activated. If you're setting up a blog, click the "Blog" category at the top. For each theme, you can click on the "Demo" link to see how the site could look with that theme. You can see that some of the themes are for purchase; I'd wait and play around with WordPress before making any decision on a premium theme at this stage. Once you've chosen the theme you want to start with, click the "Use this Theme" button. (It's easy to change themes again— in fact it's even a good idea to play around with a few to see what the options are.)

8. You can now customize your theme, but there are things you should understand about how WordPress works before this makes much sense, so I wouldn't choose the option to customize the theme right away. Instead, I would first go to the WordPress.com admin (click the "x" at the top right of the window). The WordPress admin is fairly complex as there are many options available to you, and you'll get to know it well as you work on your blog, but here's a basic tour. On the following page we'll look at the different areas of the WordPress.com admin.

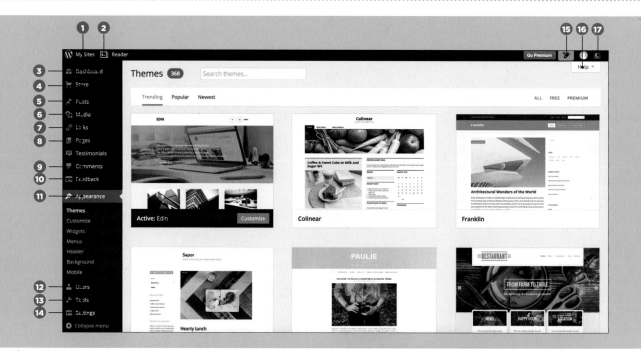

1. Clicking on the "My Sites" button and then on "View Site" allows you to see the public face of the website. If you have several sites, you can switch between them here.

2. Read other people's blog posts and find other blogs in your areas of interest.

3. Within the dashboard area, you can check on your website stats (how many people are visiting) and look at comments you've posted on other people's blogs across the WordPress.com network.

4. Add a domain, set up your email, or upgrade your package (to remove ads, add a custom design facility, etc.). You can also purchase premium themes from here.

5. Add posts to your blog. See the facing page for the "New Post" interface in detail.

6. The Media Library is where the images you upload to your site are stored.

7. Add links to other blogs, websites, etc. to be displayed in a widget in your sidebar.

8. This is where you create static pages such as your "About" page and your "Contact" page (as distinct from blog posts).

9. This is where you manage comments left on your blog by other readers.

10. This is where you reply to messages sent to you from a contact form on your website.

11. The Appearance area is where you change themes, customize your theme, and switch on a mobile theme if your theme isn't already responsive. From here, you also arrange the items in your menu bar, and set up your widgets. Widgets are elements in the sidebar (side column) of your website.

12. Add other users and assign them different roles, change passwords, change the color scheme of the admin area, and input

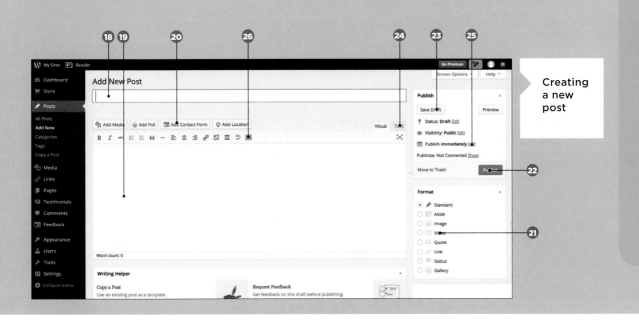

Creating a new post

information about users, including how names appear when you post on the blog.

13. Enable a "Post by email" feature, plus validate a connection with other services.

14. Change your blog title, tagline, and time zone. Configure your social media sharing buttons (under "Sharing") and open your blog to the search engines (under "Reading" > "Site Visibility"). Choose whether you want your blog posts to appear on the front page, or a static page (for example, a "Home" page), under "Reading" > "Front page displays."

15. A quick way of posting to your blog.

16. Access account settings and the Help section.

17. A quick way to monitor comments and who's following you.

18. Type your blog post title here.

19. Type your post content here.

20. Add images, contact forms, etc. by clicking these buttons.

21. Change the format of your blog post. (Not all themes will have this option.)

22. Publish your post.

23. Save your post as a draft, which you can publish manually later.

24. If you ever need to paste in a snippet of code, paste it into the "Text" view rather than the "Visual" view.

25. Schedule a post to be published automatically at a later date.

26. Reveal more formatting buttons by clicking here.

Setting up SELF-HOSTED WORDPRESS

Before you can install WordPress to your website, you need first to be sure that you have successfully connected your domain name to your hosting, as shown back on page 19. If this is done successfully, you will see your hosting company's holding page when you visit your website.

How exactly you install WordPress depends on your host, but as you will have chosen a host with a simple install system, it should be easy, and will not be too different from either of the setups pictured below.

If your hosting company is Bluehost, the installation process will look something like this (although the interface may change slightly from time to time).

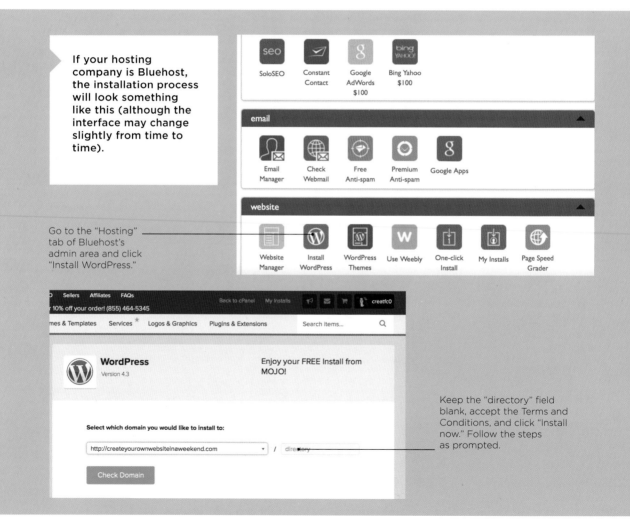

Go to the "Hosting" tab of Bluehost's admin area and click "Install WordPress."

Keep the "directory" field blank, accept the Terms and Conditions, and click "Install now." Follow the steps as prompted.

If you have any difficulty installing WordPress with your host, check the "help" area, or ask them for assistance. When you've completed your install, keep your login details safely.

MAKE SURE YOUR LOGIN IS SECURE

Don't choose "admin" as your WordPress username as this can make your site unsecure, and choose a strong password. Your host may insist that you choose a complicated password. Even if they don't, create one using numbers, capital letters, and special symbols. This is very important for the security of your site.

Go to "Goodies" > "One-Click Installs" in the navigation and click on "WordPress."

If your hosting company is DreamHost, the setup will look something like this.

Leave this field blank and click "Install it for me now." Check your email, click the "Install" link in the email you receive, and follow the steps as prompted.

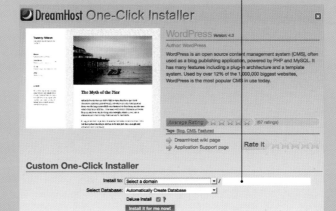

GETTING STARTED WITH WORDPRESS

Your live WordPress site is at http://www.yourdomain.com. The admin area, in which you will customize your new website and add content to it, is at http://www.yourdomain.com/wp-admin. It can be useful to work within two separate tabs within your browser window, as shown opposite, or you can switch backward and forward using links on the dark grey strip at the top, which is only visible on the live site when you're logged in (no-one else can see it). You make changes to the site from within the admin area, then you visit the live site to see the changes; if you can't see the changes, refresh (or "reload") the browser window—you can do this by clicking on the little circular arrow to the right of the field in which you can see the web address.

Follow these first steps before you start building your site:

1. Switch to the theme you want to use. If you want to play around with some basic themes to get used to WordPress, try out the free themes that come installed with WordPress (go to "Appearance" > "Themes"), or add new themes from the WordPress Free Themes Directory "Appearance" > "Themes" > "Add New." If you're adding a premium theme, upload the zip file via "Appearance" > "Themes" > "Add New" > "Upload Theme." Upload, and then activate the theme, so that it goes live. (See page 104–105 for some good places to find premium WordPress themes.)

2. Go to "Settings" > "General" and add an optional subheading for your site, and change the time zone.

3. Go to "Settings" > "Reading" and select the checkbox that says "Discourage search engines from indexing this site" while you are building your website; make sure you uncheck it when your site is ready to go live. (You don't want people to find your site in Google when you're nowhere near ready to go public.)

4. Go to "Settings" > "Discussion" and deselect the checkbox that says "Allow people to post comments on new articles" while you are building the pages of your website (you won't usually want people to be able to leave comments on your website pages). Select this again when you are ready to start posting on your blog, because you do want people to be able to leave comments at the bottom of your blog posts. (This is just a short cut to save you some time as you build your site; this setting can be overridden on each individual page or post.)

5. Go to "Users" > "Your Profile" and decide how you are going to be named when you post on your blog. (You can change the color scheme of the admin area while you're here, though no one else will see it.)

6. Go to "Settings" > "Permalinks" and select the radio button next to "Post name." This means that the web pages generated by WordPress as you create your site will have web addresses that mean something to the search engines. (Don't spend any time worrying what I mean by this—it's just more useful.)

Live site | Admin

The live site is in the left tab and the admin area is in the right.

SITE SECURITY

You must keep your WordPress site updated in order to keep it secure. It's also essential that you set up a backup system for your WordPress site, and save copies of your site to your computer as well as to your host. See page 167 for some recommendations.

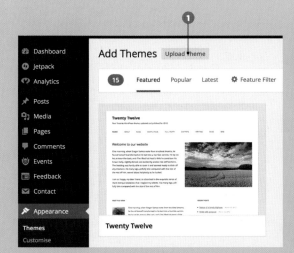

Above: **To add a premium theme, go to "Appearance" > "Themes" > "Add New" > and click the "Upload Theme" button. Navigate to and select the zip file; you then install and activate the theme.**

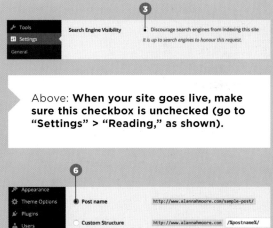

Above: **When your site goes live, make sure this checkbox is unchecked (go to "Settings" > "Reading," as shown).**

Above: **Make sure you select the "Post name" option from within the "Settings" > "Permalinks" area; this gives your web pages addresses that are meaningful to the search engines. Do this before you start creating your pages and blog posts.**

When you first install WordPress, they give you some links to get you started which you can see on the admin area's main page. By all means fiddle around with these to help you get familiar with the system, but you also need an overall understanding of what happens where:

1. This is where you change themes. Within this area you also manage your menus, as well as your "widgets"—these are elements you can put in the sidebar or footer of your website, such as a search box, links to your latest blog posts, a Twitter feed, etc. Note that within the "Appearance" area you can also make some customizations to your website, but when you install a premium theme, it will most likely have its own customization section that will appear in the navigation, usually at the bottom, once you've installed it.

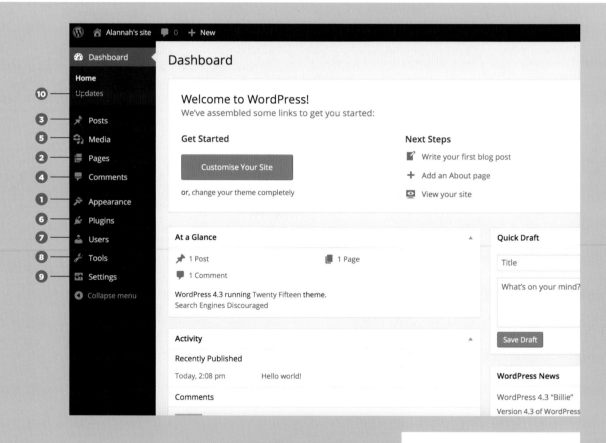

Here's a basic tour around the WordPress admin area.

2. This is where you add pages to your website. Once you've created and saved the pages, go to "Appearance" > "Menus" and create a menu (you need to specify where you want that menu to appear); you can then add the new pages to the menu and reorder them as you like.

3. This is where you write your blog posts for the site (see the tip box if you don't want your blog posts displayed on the front page of your site). You can (optionally) group your posts into categories, and assign tags to them (which function like keywords).

4. This is where you moderate and reply to comments posted to your site.

5. This is where the images you upload to the site will reside (although you'll most usually be adding them to your site directly via your page content). This section is called "Media" and in theory you can upload video and audio there as well, though in fact using YouTube, Vimeo or SoundCloud looks way better than uploading directly to WordPress. You simply paste the "Share" link from any of these straight into the text area of your page (on a line of its own) and the video or audio element will magically appear.

6. This is where you add plugins to your site. Plugins are extras you can add to WordPress to make it do other things—for example, showing a list of events, or turning it into an online store. (See Chapter 13 for details of some plugins you can add to WordPress).

7. This is where you can add other users, and determine what you'll allow them to do on the site (add posts, edit other posts, etc.). You can generate new passwords and fill in your profile (some themes will display a profile of the users who post on the blog).

8. You should add a backup tool to your WordPress installation (see page 167); this is where you'll access it.

9. Inside the "Settings" area you can change the title and subtitle of the site, change the time zone and the administrative email address, determine the page that displays on the front page, and remove the block to the search engines (these last two under "Reading"); you can also modify your "Comments" settings (inside "Discussion").

10. You'll see a number here if there are updates to your WordPress site. You need to make sure you keep it updated at all times in order for it to be secure.

DO YOU WANT YOUR BLOG TO APPEAR ON YOUR HOME PAGE?

The default setting is for your blog posts to be displayed on your home page. If you want a home page rather than your blog to appear on the front page of your website, first create a home page and a blog page (within the "Pages" area; you can name them "Home" and "Blog" or "News"—or whatever you like), then navigate to "Settings" > "Reading"; check the box next to "A static page" and select the page you want to be your home page. Then, next to "Posts page," choose the page you have created to be your blog page, and click the "Save Changes" button. (Only your blog posts will appear on this page, so there's no point writing anything there.)

Setting up STRIKINGLY

Before you begin working on your Strikingly website, it will certainly help you to first check out the websites other people have built on the Strikingly showcase at https://www. strikingly.com/s/discover. You'll be able to see what's possible, and create a sketch of how you'd like your own site to be laid out, before you jump in and start designing from within the system.

To get set up, simply enter your name and email address on the home page (or sign in via Facebook—it won't post anything there). Choose a template to get started—which one you choose isn't a big deal, as you can easily change at the next step. When you sign in you'll be offered to take a "tour"—this is fast to do, and shows you around, so I recommend you do it. Here's how the interface works:

1. Change the style (color scheme and, for some templates, the font as well) of the current template, or the template itself.

2. Toggle between different layouts for the individual section here.

3. Reorder your website sections here. (The sections are simply the horizontal elements that display your website content, as you can see in the screenshot opposite.)

4. Add new sections here, including a blog, store, social media feed, or elements from their App Store.

5. Connect to your domain here; add search engine information, Google Analytics (see page 164) and mobile-specific actions (call, find directions, etc.; Pro only).

6. Hover over text or click "Background" to change text and background images.

7. Click here to publish your changes.

8. Get help from a real person here.

You can easily upgrade to Pro (and remove the Strikingly branding) by clicking any of the yellow "Upgrade" buttons you'll come across in the admin area as you explore your way around it; there's a 14-day trial period for paid plans which will let you see if the system can offer you everything you need. (Note that a paid Limited account allows you to connect your domain, but your site will still show the Strikingly branding; to remove it, you'll need to choose the Pro package.)

BUILD A SITE FROM FACEBOOK OR LINKEDIN

If you want to start your site from your Facebook or LinkedIn, click the "one-click" links at the bottom of the page, when you're logged in but not editing. This can be a good starting point from which to kick off a personal profile website, if you haven't yet worked out quite how you'd like your information to be displayed.

Below: **Here's how the Strikingly admin interface appears.**

Left: **Use the App Store to add a MailChimp newsletter signup form, Google map, Eventbrite widget, and many other add-ons.**

Setting up WEEBLY

Sign up from the home page. Choose from the "Site," "Blog" and "Store" options, and choose a theme to get started with. You'll be asked to register a domain name, or connect a domain you already own, but you don't need this yet; you can connect a domain later when your site is ready to go live, and in the meantime, publish to a Weebly subdomain.

You'll now be taken to the editing area. The interface works like this:

1. Here is where you add elements to the pages. Simply drag the items from the left hand area onto the page where you want them, and move them around; click any element on the page to edit it. When you create a new page, you can either drag in elements, or you can click "Choose a Layout" and select from some pre-set page layouts, designed to work with different kinds of pages. Navigate around the site to work on the different pages simply by clicking the page titles in the menu.

2. Here is where you choose from a selection of pre-defined color schemes, change fonts and change your background image—there's a large selection on offer, or you can upload your own.

3. Here's where you add new pages, re-order the navigation, and under the "Advanced" heading, you can add in search engine settings for the individual pages (we'll see more about this in Chapter 11).

4. If you're implementing an online store on your site, here's where you add your products and manage your orders.

5. Here's where you configure various site-wide settings: global search engine settings, site title, blog settings, and add other site editors.

6. Here's where you access the support center.

7. Toggle between mobile view and desktop view here. If the template is responsive, as is the case with this one, you don't need to make adjustments within the mobile view.

8. This is the button to click when you're ready to go live. Don't worry if you publish too early and you then change your mind—you can unpublish again (go to "Settings" > "General" and scroll down to the bottom and you'll see an "Unpublish" button. This can come in handy if you connect your domain and then realize you aren't ready for people to see your site.

9. Gives you access to your account, your website stats and the place where you can connect your domain and set up email.

10. Here's where you upgrade your account —you need to do this in order to connect your domain.

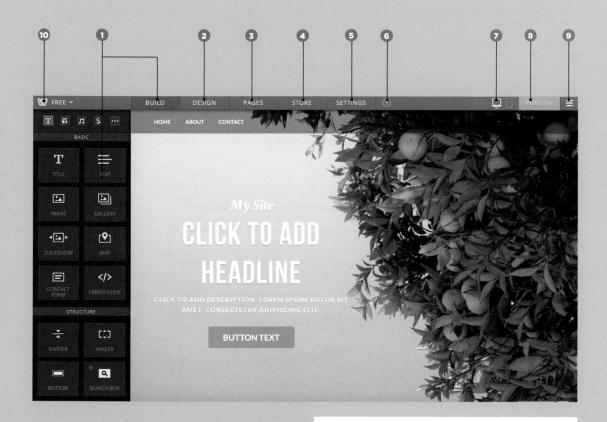

The Weebly interface.

Setting up WIX

As usual, you start with Wix by signing up from the home page. With Wix, it's really crucial that you get the right template before you start building your site in earnest. You can change, but you will have to start your site from scratch. There is nothing stopping you messing around with a few different templates before you properly begin—you'll have to start afresh each time—but it will probably help if you spend some time browsing the template store in advance, and also looking at the live examples (click the "Explore" tab at the top of the main website); for each site shown, you can see which template has been used.

Once you've decided which template to use, click the "Edit" button. Once inside the editing area, the interface works like this:

1. Click the different areas of the page to change them. Here, I've clicked the images, in order to change the pictures in the gallery. Clicking the different circular buttons offers you different options—for the gallery we can see (circular buttons left to right) general settings options, layout options, design options and animation options.

2. Clicking on each element on the page will bring up a "Help" button, which explains how to edit that element.

3. From here, you can navigate through the site to edit the different pages. You don't have to stick with the pages in the dummy setup. You can easily delete them as shown in the lower screenshot (a), add new pages (b) and drag them around so they're ordered differently in the menu (c). You can hide pages from the menu (d) or show them as submenu items ("dropdowns"—e).

4. Change the background of the page you're currently working on here (you can apply the background to all pages at the same time). Wix gives you loads of free images; you can also add your own images or purchase others. They also have a selection of videos that you can use as backgrounds.

5. Add elements to the page you're working on here (text, image, blog, store, etc.). When you add elements, you can simply move them around the page with your mouse, and grab the edges to resize them. The page area will enlarge to accommodate new items.

6. Add extras (newsletter signup forms, comments, live chat) from the App Market (free and paid-for).

7. Manage your uploads here—images, audio, and documents.

8. Edit the mobile version of your website here.

9. Preview your site here.

10. Upgrade here to remove Wix branding and connect your domain.

11. Undo and redo buttons mean if you make a mistake you can easily remove it.

12. When you're ready, you can publish your site.

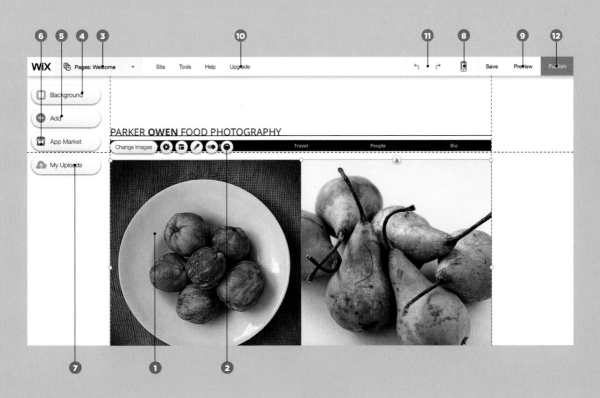

Above: **The Wix editing interface.**

Left: **Editing options for different pages.**

Setting up
SQUARESPACE

Sign up from the home page, and pick a template to get started with. Which you choose doesn't matter much as you can easily switch later on. Go through the few questions they ask and you'll find yourself in the editing area. The basics of the editing area are as follows:

1. Mouse over each element to edit it. Shown here: editing for the home page in general, and for the different elements in the top section of the long home page. Before you can edit their dummy content, you need to first create a page that's identical to the demo. When prompted, just click the "Create" button, then the "Save" button, and a "real" page will replace the demo that you can then edit. You need to do this for all the dummy pages (and the different sections within the long home page).

2. Navigate around the pages of the site to edit them. (Click on the page you want to edit, then mouse over the element, then click "Edit".) (You can also navigate around the site, in order to edit the pages, via the menu.) You don't have to keep the pages they provide you with; to delete a page, mouse over it and click the trash icon, as shown in the lower screenshot (a). To add a page, click the "Add Page" button (b)—the new page can be positioned in the menu by simply dragging it to the right position in the list of pages on the left, or you can add it as a section on the long home page attaching it, simply by dragging, into the "tree" structure of the home page (c). You can add other elements (gallery, shop, blog, etc.) by clicking the "+" sign (d). To add content, click on "Edit" (e); mouse over the text area and click on one of the gray "teardrop"-shaped indicators (which they call an "Insert Point," shown in the smaller screenshot—f) to bring up a box. Choose from here the element that you want to add; once you've created some elements, you can drag them next to each other to create columns, if you want to.

3. Make site-wide changes to the site design (fonts, colors, etc.) and change templates here. When you switch templates, you first have to install the new template, then preview it, then set it as the live template.

4. Enter your description for the search engines for each page here (as explained in Chapter 11).

5. Set up an e-commerce store here.

6. Check your website statistics here.

7. Manage your blog comments here.

8. Connect your domain and set up your email here; connect social media accounts.

9. Access Squarespace help here—I recommend you watch the series of "Getting Started" videos.

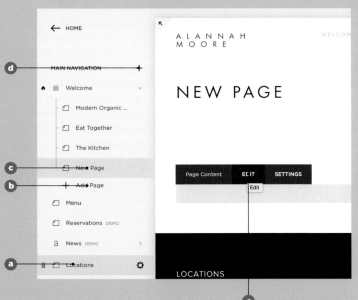

The Squarespace interface and editing options.

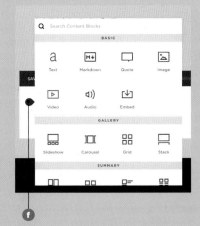

Setting up SHOPIFY

Sign up from the home page. When asked whether you want to set up an online store or a retail store/popup shop, choose "Online Store" for now. Answer the series of questions (you can change these details later).

Shopify gives you a series of steps to get up and running quickly. Here's an overview of how the system works:

1. Choose your theme. You start with a basic theme installed—it's quite clean and nice-looking, but chances are you will want something a little more sophisticated. It's easy to change themes—any work you've done on a particular theme is saved even if you switch themes, and it's easy to change back again. Click on "Online Store" then "Themes," then click the "Visit Theme Store" button. You can browse the available themes, both free and premium. When you've chosen your theme, click the green "Install" button; you can choose to install it live now, or publish it later from the "Themes" area of your admin area. You can also purchase premium themes from the Theme Store. Upload the zip file by clicking the "Upload theme" button in the "Themes" area. You customize your theme from this area as well (click the blue "Customize theme" button), but you'll want to add some products first (3). When you've added your products, you can create extra pages (About, Terms and Conditions, Returns, etc.), optionally also create a blog for your site, and group all these pages into menus (main menu and footer), again back here within the "Online Store" area.

2. View your online store here.

3. Add your products here. Inside this area you also group them into "Collections," decide which ones will show up on the front page, manage your inventory, and create gift cards.

4. Your orders will be listed here.

5. Manage your customers here.

6. Analyze your products, orders, payments, traffic, etc. here.

7. Set up discount codes here.

8. Add extras from the App Store here (some are free and some premium): newsletter signups, recurring billing, loyalty programs, live chat, order fulfillment, etc.

9. Within the "Settings" area, configure your payment, tax, and shipping details, and adjust the wording of the emails customers will receive on setting up an account, making an order, etc. Here is also where you can add a "Point-of-Sale" channel, which enables you to sell in person via iPhone or iPad. Connect with Google Analytics and set your search engine description. Finally, before you can launch your store, "unlock" your site by picking a paid plan; you can do this either within the "Settings area" (choose the "Online Store" tab), or within the "Online Store" area (1).

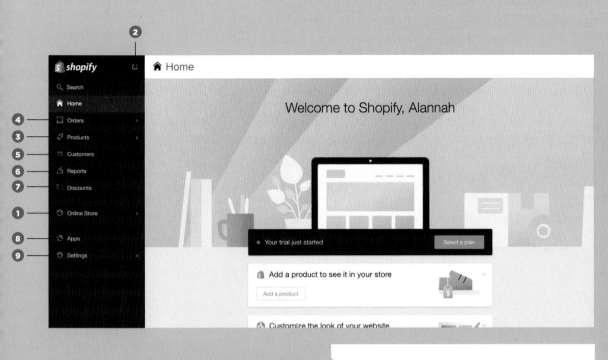

The Shopify interface.

Customizing a theme is easy to do—go to "Online Store" > "Themes" and click the "Customize Theme" button. You can change colors and fonts, add your logo, add images to a slideshow, decide which products to display on the front page, set your social media buttons, and so on.

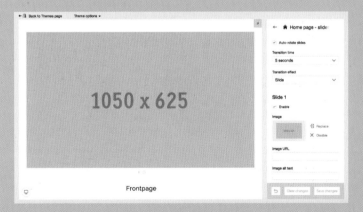

Setting up WOOCOMMERCE

As we've said, there are a number of different plugins you can use to transform your WordPress site into a fully functioning online store. The most popular one is currently WooCommerce. To use it, you need a WooCommerce-compatible theme. The makers of WooCommerce create beautiful themes—take a look at WooThemes.com—but you don't need to use one of their themes; there are many themes by other makers (see page 104) that are designed specifically for use with WooCommerce.

For demonstration purposes, we are going to use the basic free online store theme by WooThemes called Storefront; this theme can be added directly from the WordPress Free Themes Directory (by going to "Appearance" > "Themes" > "Add New" and searching "Storefront" in the search box). (You may be adding a premium theme from WooThemes or elsewhere—this you do by purchasing and downloading the zip file containing the new theme; you then upload it via "Themes" > "Add New" > "Upload Theme," and activate it.)

Navigate to the new "Storefront" area that you now have inside the "Appearance" area. Scroll down a little as shown opposite, click the button labeled "Install WooCommerce," and activate the plugin when it's installed. (If you have uploaded a premium theme, you'll need to install the WooCommerce plugin the way that one normally installs plugins. Go to "Plugins" > "Add New" and search for "WooCommerce" in the search box. Install it, and activate it.)

If you install WooCommerce from the special Storefront page, it provides you with a very easy-to-use step-by-step setup—just follow the screen prompts as instructed. (You can edit all the information you put in here later, if you need to.) When you're done, click the purple "Create Your First Product" button. You're now ready to go, uploading your product details, descriptions, prices, etc. to the site. If you've installed WooCommerce the normal way, via the "Plugins" area, you'll have to configure it via the "WooCommerce" > "Settings" screen.

Here's a quick tour around the WordPress interface now that WooCommerce is installed:

1. Here's where you add your products, product photos, and product categories.

2. Monitor your orders here, check your reports, set up coupons and manage your settings (tax, payment systems, shipping etc.—shown here).

3. Customize your "Storefront" theme here (depending on the theme you've chosen, your customization area may appear in a different place in the navigation).

4. Access a WooThemes setup video here, plus support documentation.

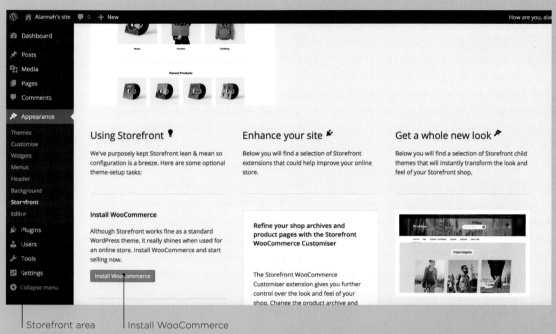

Storefront area | Install WooCommerce

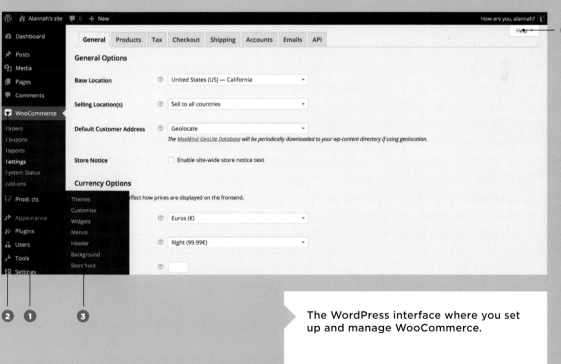

The WordPress interface where you set up and manage WooCommerce.

Setting up EMAIL ADDRESSES

Ideally, you need an email address that matches your website address (that is, yourname@yourdomain.com). Some platforms will allow you to create a "forward," which is an email address that looks like a matching email address—yourname@yourdomain.com—but it functions only to send messages sent to that email address to another email address (for example, your gmail, hotmail, or yahoo address).

A better answer, and the one that most of the platforms suggest, is to set up a matching email address with Google Apps for Work (https://www.google.com/work/apps/ business/); at the time of writing the cost of this is $50 per year. An alternative this is Zoho (https://www.zoho.com), which provides email for one domain for free, and also has its own suite of tools and a premium pricing structure if you require more than 5GB of storage space.

Before you commit to one or the other, read the information concerning setting up email addresses provided by your chosen platform. They usually have clear instructions on how to set up, and it may be more straightforward to do so from within their interface; they may also have pricing deals, and they may even have new partnerships with alternative providers that have come into existence since the time of writing.

If you're using self-hosted WordPress, you'll have your own hosting setup, so it's a simple matter to set up your matching email addresses via their interface. They'll provide you with instructions on how to configure your email software—Mail, Outlook, or whatever it is that you normally use on your computer or your smartphone. Or you might want to pay extra and sign up for Google Apps so that you can use the Gmail browser-based interface.

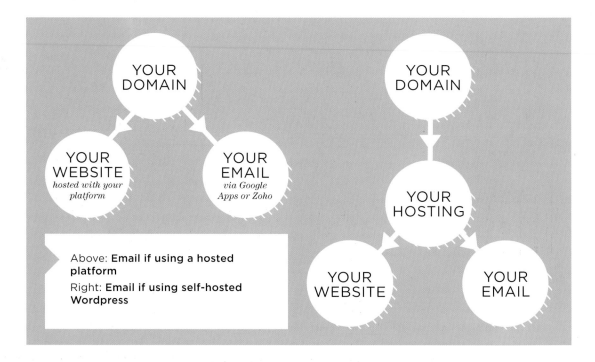

YOUR DOMAIN

YOUR WEBSITE
hosted with your platform

YOUR EMAIL
via Google Apps or Zoho

YOUR DOMAIN

YOUR HOSTING

YOUR WEBSITE

YOUR EMAIL

Above: **Email if using a hosted platform**

Right: **Email if using self-hosted Wordpress**

A DANGEROUS BUSINESS
SELF-HOSTED WORDPRESS

USA   HTTP://WWW.DANGEROUS-BUSINESS.COM

"WordPress is such a fantastic tool for bloggers. It can seem overwhelming at first, but once you start poking around you'll realize that it's all pretty easy to figure out. WordPress is also great because it means you can purchase and install ready-made themes from lots of places across to web and have your site ready to go in no time.

My biggest piece of advice is to start out with a self-hosted site. This will save you trying to migrate over from a free WordPress or Blogger site later, which can be a big pain. You might initially balk at the idea of spending money on a blog. But if you have any intention of taking it seriously, self-hosted is the way to go!

I would make sure you have a clear vision of what you want your blog to be before you dive in. Figure out things like your theme, what you'll write about, and what will be the hook that will help you stand out from the millions of other blogs out there. You don't need to rush into it!"

Amanda Williams

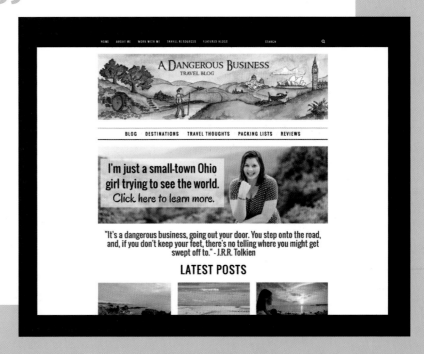

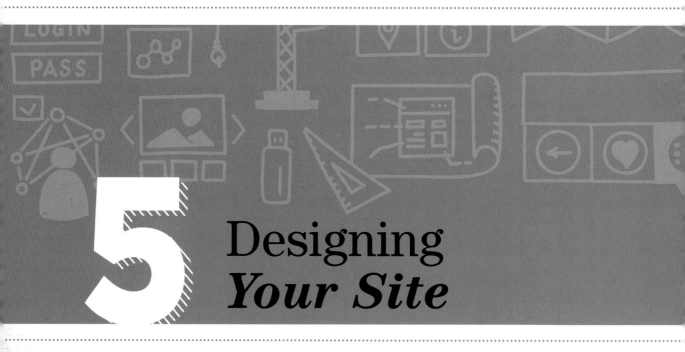

5 Designing *Your Site*

Working with TEMPLATES

You're armed with your website plan, you've decided which platform to use, and you've perhaps played around with it a bit to see how it works—now it's time to start building your site in earnest.

Unless you're using Wix and you choose to use their "Start from scratch" blank template, you're not going to actually *design* your website; you'll be working within the framework of a ready-designed template (or "theme"). But make no mistake, the design choices that you make at this stage can make or break your website, no matter how brilliant your content is. Content is certainly the most important aspect of a website, but if it doesn't look good, then your whole venture could lack credibility.

First of all, you need to make sure you choose the right template—one that will do everything you need it to do, and will look the way it should look in order to appeal to your target market. It can be confusing to choose a template, which is why it pays to have thought out your pages, and what you want to include on your pages, in advance. Your template needs to bow to your needs—not the other way around. Look at the page overleaf for some guidelines that will help you when you're making this very important decision.

Once you've decided on your template, you'll want to make some tweaks to make it look more individual, and so that it matches your branding. You may want to change the background, adjust the color scheme and perhaps change the fonts as well. Even a few simple, well-judged changes can give the site instant personality.

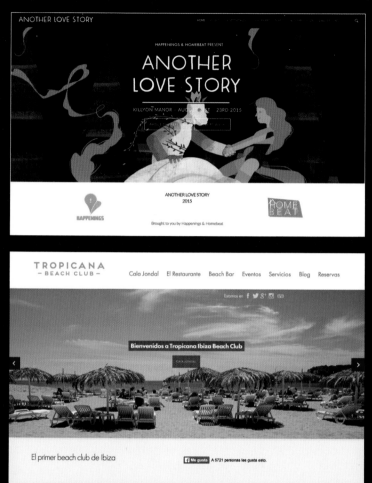

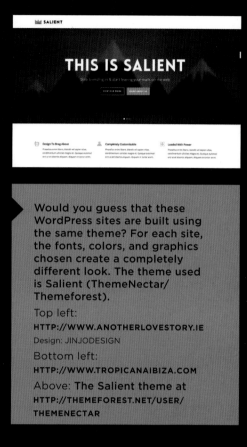

Would you guess that these WordPress sites are built using the same theme? For each site, the fonts, colors, and graphics chosen create a completely different look. The theme used is Salient (ThemeNectar/Themeforest).

Top left:
HTTP://WWW.ANOTHERLOVESTORY.IE
Design: JINJODESIGN

Bottom left:
HTTP://WWW.TROPICANAIBIZA.COM

Above: The Salient theme at
HTTP://THEMEFOREST.NET/USER/
THEMENECTAR

Note that the level of customization available to you will depend on the system you are using, and then sometimes on the template as well. Users of Strikingly and Weebly will be obliged to choose from just a few preset color palettes rather than using their own choice, though you do get a selection of fonts. With WordPress, take a careful look at the wording to see if you can make the changes you want to with your chosen template.

DISPLAYING YOUR CONTENT

Chunks of plain text can be boring on a web page and aren't really inviting for the site visitor. Think how you can lay out your text for maximum clarity and visual interest; look at other websites and see how they use headers, boxes, bands of color and buttons to divide the page. Many templates offer special content elements that display testimonials, show information about team members, divide text into tabs, and so on—make use of these, according to the style of your website.

Some Tips to Help You Choose a Template

- Take your time over it. Choosing a template can seem like a big task, but it seems less so if you assign plenty of time to it.

- Be methodical—take notes and screenshots, and make sketches of suitable layouts. This will help you identify the templates that could work for you.

- Make sure you're looking at the right kind of website template—if you're setting up an online magazine, look at magazine templates; if you need a portfolio, look at portfolio templates. Don't choose a template just because it looks cool and you like it—it needs to suit your purpose.

- Check whether it has the features that you need: for example, a portfolio to display your work, e-commerce to sell your products. Make sure that these work in the way that you want them to; for a portfolio, for example, you may need to group the elements into projects, and add a text explanation, whereas not every portfolio setup enables you to do this. For e-commerce too there are many different ways of displaying items.

- Establish whether you can make any layout changes you might need to make. This doesn't apply to platforms such as Wix or Squarespace which allow you to move everything around. But some WordPress themes don't let you change the position of certain elements, and most Shopify themes are quite rigid in layout. With WordPress, if you want to change the way things appear on the demo website, you're ideally looking for a theme that has a drag-and-drop interface, with "Visual Composer" being the most popular; many modern themes use a system like this, but it isn't a given, so you'll need to read the description carefully.

- Similarly, if you want to change the fonts and colors, make sure that you are able to.

- Check whether the theme is responsive (see page 31). Some older templates may not be.

- With WordPress, a good way of getting started is to use the dummy content from the demo, which you can then adjust to suit you. Find out if you can obtain the content which you can then upload to your own website; the documentation provided will usually give you instructions as to how to do this. (Be aware that you probably won't have the right to use the images.)

POLYAMOROUS ART
SELF-HOSTED WORDPRESS

FRANCE   **HTTP://WWW.POLYAMOROUSART.COM**

"Buy a really great professionally made theme that uses Visual Composer. Also, spend your money on great stock photos, even if it's just a few of them; they're worth it. Really, they make all the difference.

I consider websites works-in-progress; that takes away a lot of pressure to make the "perfect" thing, because when you're trapped by perfectionism it can prevent you from getting things done."

Sarah Arlen

COLORS

Colors for websites are described by using what's called a "hex code." When you're adjusting the colors for your website, you'll typically be asked to name the color you want by providing the hex code. This is a series of six numbers or letters (occasionally three); for example, black is #000000 and white is #FFFFFF.

You may have heard of "web-safe colors." A few years ago, these were colors that we could be sure would show up correctly on a computer screen; this is no longer an issue, however, as modern screens can display millions of different shades—so you can now pick whichever colors you like for your website and not worry about restrictions.

How do you find out the hex code for a color? It's easy—go to http://www.colorpicker.com, choose your color, and copy the code. If you're using Wix, you'll find it contains an inbuilt color picker; alternatively, if you use Pixlr—see the next chapter—you can easily pick colors and get their hex codes using the inbuilt color selector.

DECIDING WHICH COLORS TO USE

Changing the colors on your website is one way to add life and instant individuality, but you want to make sure you choose colors that work.

You shouldn't choose too many colors for your website—three should do for most. One will be your background—a neutral color, say white, or light beige, or an ultra-light gray. Then you'll want a strong, prominent color that you might use for your headings. A third color, which may contrast with this, you could use for accents—perhaps for text links and buttons. If you need more colors—which you may, for example for content boxes or outlines—you can use lighter or darker shades of either your second or third color. (We're not counting the color of your regular text here—this will most usually be preset to a dark gray that looks almost black.)

You can get ideas for a palette for your website by surfing around the web, or you can visit http://www.colourlovers.com/palettes—

Here's the hex code for this color.

Move up and down the slider to the right to choose an approximate color, then refine your choice within the larger square; the hex code for the color you've chosen is shown above the square.

WWW.COLORPICKER.COM

here you can get ideas on which colors look great together, and you can see what's on-trend by browsing the "Most Loved" and "Most Favorites" tabs.

You could make a selection for a website from the palette shown in the screenshot according to the three-colors guideline, as follows:

1. A neutral color for the background. You could choose white, or try a very pale variation of the third color in the palette.

2. One of the turquoises, for your primary prominent color; let's choose the second.

3. One of the oranges, to contrast with that, as an accent color; let's choose the brightest.

4. If you need another color for boxes, etc., let's use a paler shade of turquoise.

PICKING COLORS FROM YOUR BROWSER WINDOW

The free ColorZilla add-on for Firefox is a really useful tool that uses an "eyedropper" to pick colors from anywhere within your website browser. When you click, it saves the hex code to the clipboard and you can then paste the code somewhere or note it down.
HTTP://WWW.COLORZILLA.COM

The hex codes are shown for each of the colors as indicated (within the Palettes section of the http://www.colourlovers.com website).

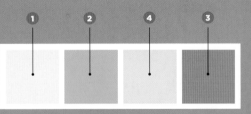

So, your palette might look like this.

When you've chosen your colors, note down the codes so that you can set them from within your admin area.

#684C38 #B88E55 #F89149 #F4DF7A #DCE5C5

> Color Hunter is a useful tool that lets you create a color palette from a photograph. The system generates a palette of colors, from which you can pick two or three to create variations.
>
> HTTP://COLORHUNTER.COM

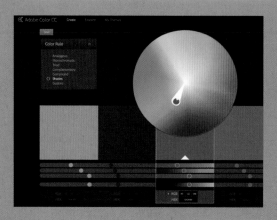

> Adobe Color can generate shade variations of different colors, as well as other combinations.
>
> HTTPS://COLOR.ADOBE.COM

USING PHOTOGRAPHS AS A COLOR BASE

One way of deciding which colors to use for your site is by taking them from a photograph. If you have an image that's going to have a permanent, prominent place on your site then it could be a good idea to base your colors around that image. Go to http://colorhunter.com, upload your photo, and you have a ready palette of colors to choose from. (A more sophisticated alternative is http://www.colourlovers.com/photocopa.)

ASSOCIATIONS ATTACHED TO COLORS

Of course, you need to decide on a color scheme that is appropriate for the field you are in. There are no absolutely fixed rules, but certain colors have certain associations. For example, blue is often seen as trustworthy, conservative, and safe, which makes it a common choice for banks and businesses. This list may help you decide on a basic color to base your site around:

- **Red**—strength, passion, heat, excitement, power. (To be used with caution on a website—it can be very overpowering.)
- **Orange**—fun, youth, playfulness, vitality.
- **Yellow**—optimism, happiness.
- **Green**—everything ecological, health, serenity, freshness, nature, relaxation.
- **Blue**—dependability, stability, safety, trustworthiness.
- **Purple**—intelligence, luxury, individuality, eccentricity, creativity, royalty.
- **Pink**—energy, youth, girliness, prettiness, romance.
- **Black**—power, drama, luxury, mystery.
- **Gray**—calm, neutrality, balance.
- **White**—cleanliness, simplicity, purity.
- **Brown**—reliability, earthiness, nature.

FONTS

Your website will typically use three fonts (maybe even just two): one for the page titles, one for headings (these may be the same), and one for the regular page text. You don't want to incorporate more than this or your pages will look confused and cluttered.

If you want to add character to your site, you can replace the page title font or the heading font with one that's more unusual (see below), but always keep the regular page text font simple—it needs to be easily legible.

CHOOSING FONTS

Squarespace has a massive collection of fonts you can use—600 Google fonts and 1000 Typekit fonts! (Typekit is a service from Adobe that you usually have to pay to use.) To save you going through all the fonts in search of the right ones, they have a curated selection that you can easily pick from. With other systems, you won't get quite such a range; with Wix and Strikingly the selection is pared down, and with WordPress it depends on the theme. You can easily see what a font looks like by going to the Google fonts page (https://www.google.com/fonts/) or to the Typekit library (https://typekit.com/fonts).

CODYSTAR IS A FONT WITH CHARACTER
Cabin Sketch is fun as well.

Garamond is an example of a "Serif" font.
Open Sans is an example of a "Sans Serif" font.

Top: **Distinctive fonts used for page titles or headings can give instant personality to a site.**

Above: **Open Sans and Garamond are two clean and easy-to-read examples of fonts often used for regular page text. "Serif"** fonts such as Garamond—serif simply means the letters have little "tails"—are more traditional in feel and can look more classy; "sans serif" fonts (without tails) look cleaner and more modern.

Right: **Font Pair is a good place to find successful font combinations.**

HTTP://FONTPAIR.CO
Created by Mills Digital.

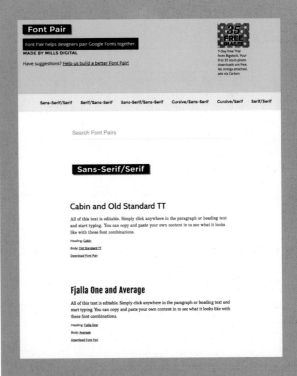

Some Design Mistakes to Avoid

- Too many colors—cut them down to three, plus variants. Avoid using two or three primary colors together, and don't change the color of your text.

- Don't change fonts frequently. Stick with just a couple. Don't introduce a new font suddenly, even for emphasis.

- Don't center everything. Large titles or important statements are often centered, but chunks of text, and their sub-headings, are usually left-aligned.

- Avoid chunks of text that go the full width of your website—this is hard to read. Put a wide margin on either side.

- Avoid too-small text as this can't be read easily. But don't display all your text in header-size lettering, either!

- Don't clutter your pages. Plenty of space around the different elements makes the pages more legible.

- Don't stretch, or squash, images. Keep their proportions and resize them, if necessary, before putting them on your website.

- If your website layout requires large images, make sure yours are large enough. If a picture is fuzzy, or doesn't fill the space required, choose one with larger pixel measurements (see the next chapter).

- Including lots of different logos (for example press logos) of different sizes and colors can look incoherent. Use a graphics program to make them all the same height and, optionally, convert them to "grayscale" (that is, black and white).

- Avoid too much movement on your site (e.g. with sliders). A little movement is fun and looks slick, but you don't want to distract your readers.

- Don't squash your logo. If there isn't room for it in the top strip of your website, either make the strip bigger so that there is plenty of space around the logo, or if you can't do that, don't put it in the top strip at all.

- If the background color of your website is anything other than white, you'll need your logo on a transparent background (this means it needs to be a .png file, or a .gif, rather than a .jpg). Don't display your logo on a visible white rectangle against a colored background.

- Avoid black backgrounds, unless you have a completely minimalist photography website.

THE BLISSFUL BEE
SELF-HOSTED WORDPRESS

USA | HTTP://THEBLISSFULBEE.COM

> **D**esigning a website is a lot like setting up an art gallery. You want the art to stand out, not the design of the actual gallery, which is why you typically see all white walls in a gallery.
>
> That was exactly the thought behind my blog design. The cleaner the website design was, the more my design portfolio and photography would stand out.
>
> Let your product be the attention-getter. If you over-design your website by making it distracting or cluttered, you'll probably loose the attention of your end user.

Amy Walton

Where to find WORDPRESS THEMES

There are literally thousands of WordPress themes available to .org users, created by hundreds of independent WordPress designers all over the world. Here are a few good places to start your search for the ideal theme.

ThemeForest: The largest array imaginable of WordPress themes, created by independent makers, for all types of site. Choose your category of theme (under the "WordPress" tab), or check out the "Popular" themes. (http://themeforest.net/category/wordpress)

Creative Market: Another marketplace, this one more human-sized, with a slightly more arty/designer feel than ThemeForest. You can also get photos and graphics here. (https://creativemarket.com/themes/wordpress)

Dessign: Beautiful designs for creatives. (http://dessign.net)

WooThemes: The makers of WooCommerce; they offer a range of clean, modern themes for all kinds of site (not just online stores). (http://www.woothemes.com)

ElegantThemes: The makers of the popular, super-versatile Divi theme (see the screenshot opposite). (https://www.elegantthemes.com)

StudioPress: Reliable, classic themes for all kinds of websites. (http://www.studiopress.com)

Organic Themes: A variety of themes focusing on those for creatives, bloggers and businesses, but actually, their themes can be adapted for any kind of business, as their showcase indicates; they also offer a hosted service as well. (http://organicthemes.com)

ThemeTrust: Beautiful, minimal, design-led themes for creatives and bloggers. (http://themetrust.com)

Bluchic: Soft, feminine themes for blogs and online stores. (http://www.bluchic.com)

Angie Makes: More pretty, on-trend designs created for women entrepreneurs, crafters and bloggers. (http://angiemakes.com)

WPExplorer.com: Dozens of clean, modern business themes plus a large range of free themes, many of them portfolios. This is a good place to start if you're creating a business site but don't want anything that looks too corporate. (http://www.wpexplorer.com)

Colorlib: Like WPExplorer.com, Colorlib make their own themes, including several high-quality free ones, but also provide a curated collection of themes by other makers, grouped according to theme. (https://colorlib.com)

FREE OR PREMIUM?

There are many beautiful free themes available today, and some of them are pretty flexible; if you're making a website as a fun project or an experiment, you may well find something that fits your needs. In general, though, I advise buying a premium theme—it'll be more customizable, you'll most likely be able to get support if you need it, and the cost will still be far less than getting your website built by a professional.

The WordPress Free Themes Directory:
This is connected to your WordPress admin, so you can install the themes directly from the "Themes" > "Add New" area of the interface. However it's much easier to browse the themes from the Directory, as you can click through to the makers' websites and launch a demo—this gives you a far better idea of how the theme can look once it's set up. (https://wordpress.org/themes/)

Above: **Divi** (Elegant Themes) is one of the most flexible WordPress themes around— it can be customized to suit any kind of website.
HTTP://WWW.ELEGANTTHEMES.COM/GALLERY/DIVI/

Below: **SimpleMag** (ThemesIndep, ThemeForest) is a very popular magazine-style theme with a drag-and-drop page composer.
HTTP://THEMESINDEP.COM

6 Visuals

Working with IMAGES

The visual aspect of your website is massively important. Visuals give your website life, and keep it interesting for the visitor. There are plenty of ways of giving visual interest to your site apart from just using photographs—we'll have a look at some of these in this chapter.

The three image formats used on the web are JPG (or JPEG), PNG, and GIF. The JPG format is ideal for photos, PNG is used for logos and images requiring transparency, while these days GIF is mostly used for animated graphics.

Images on the web—and this applies to photos and all other graphics—are measured in pixels (px). These are miniature dots of color. Where measurements are given, the convention is to give the width measurement first, followed by the height measurement. So, if an image is 600×450 pixels, this means it is 600 pixels wide and 450 pixels high.

Don't confuse the size of an image with the file size—"image size" means the pixel measurement, whereas the "file size" means how much space it takes up on a hard drive—kilobytes or megabytes.

It's commonly thought that "resolution" needs to 72 dpi (dots per inch) for the web. But you don't need to take any notice whatsoever of image resolution; this only matters when you're creating a document for print, such as a brochure. The only measurements that count for your website are the pixel width, and of course, the file size, since you obviously don't want a really slow-loading web page.

The solution to over-large images is to resize them before you load them up to the web. Most systems will automatically resize your images to the pixel dimensions you specify

Original

667 px
1000 px

Stretched

450 px
450 px

Correctly Resized

450 px
675 px

Correctly Cropped

450 px
450 px

The original dimensions of this image are 1000×667 pixels (1). Imagine you need a square image of 450×450 to fit within your website design. You can't just resize the image to 450×450—this changes the proportion and the "stretched" image really doesn't look good (2). Instead you first need to resize the picture so that the size is 675×450 (3), and then crop it so its width is 450 pixels (4).

for the page, but this isn't quite the same—the web page will in most cases still have to load at the entire picture size before it can show it at a smaller size. So it makes sense to resize them first—we'll see how to do that with Pixlr on page 112—and optionally also reduce the quality while saving. A minimal reduction in quality, while not noticeable on the screen, can reduce file size dramatically.

Note that images can be made smaller but never bigger (without a noticeable loss of quality), so if you buy images from a stock photo library, you must make sure you're buying them with large enough pixel dimensions for the use you have in mind; you may want to adjust the dimensions, but the images have to be big enough in the first place.

To give you an idea of pixel size, 800 pixels wide is usually the maximum width you'd ever need for an image that's part of your web page; for a full-screen background, your system or the theme you're using will normally

KEEP THE ORIGINAL IMAGE PROPORTIONS

When you're resizing an image, make sure you keep its proportions to avoid it looking stretched. If you need to change the proportions, crop the image to the right size, as shown in the above example, rather than distorting it to fit.

specify the image dimensions needed, but it won't ever be more than 2500 pixels wide, which should accommodate the largest of retina screens. In terms of file size, for a full-screen image 1 MB should be the maximum you ever use (in most cases, you'll be able to reduce the file size further); if you have several images within the body of a page, try to reduce their size to around 70 KB each.

TAKING PHOTOS
for your site

Getting professional photographs done for your website can make an enormous difference. But if this isn't possible, here are some tips to help you take your own photographs. It's obviously best if you have a good camera, but a smartphone can achieve good results as well. (If you have a lot of photographs to take, you might want to consider buying the olloclip, a wide-angle/Macro lens attachment for the iPhone; there's also the highly recommended Camera+ app, which increases performance and adds a professional touch to your iPhone photos.)

- A tripod will keep your camera (or phone) steady and enable you to use the timer to take photos that include yourself.
- Light is very important; if there is not enough, your pictures will become grainy when viewed at a larger size. Natural light is best, but if this this isn't strong enough, use additional, multiple light sources (to avoid harsh shadows). If sunlight is strong, a shade or drape will be useful in reducing glare; if you're using flash, you can tape a sheet of kitchen paper over it, to make the light softer.
- If you have a large quantity of products to photograph, it will be worth buying a light box (also called a light tent) to provide soft lighting and a consistent, professional-looking setting for the items. Or, if you feel like getting hands-on, you could try making your own. Light boxes are really simple to make using little more than a cardboard box and some cheap white fabric.

- An alternative way of giving a professional-looking seamless white background to your product shots is setting up a roll of white paper as a backdrop and horizontal surface underneath them.
- When shooting products, use the Macro button if your camera has one. This will bring the item into sharp focus, while blurring the background.
- Take multiple pictures of each setting, with small differences in angle, etc. Each will make a subtle difference and you'll be able to choose the best later on.
- Take the best quality, largest photographs that you can, and reduce the image size and file size later on. This will allow you plenty of scope to crop the images.
- Make sure your lens is clean. This is especially important if you're using a smartphone—all the bag- or pocket fluff that accumulates isn't going to do anything for your photos!

◁ An "invisible" white background is the most classic way of displaying products. Other ideas are photographing the items on a wooden or stone tabletop, on fabric, on a solid color, or with a colored backdrop. Here Australian tableware makers Hop On It have been brilliantly creative.

HTTP://WWW.HOPONIT.COM.AU

THE WINEMAKER'S LOFT
STRIKINGLY

NEW ZEALAND	HTTP://WWW.THEWINEMAKERSLOFT.CO.NZ

"We wanted a simple mobile-friendly scrolling site as travellers looking for accommodation often use mobile devices both when booking and researching. This was very important to us.

Images and photos are absolutely key. We took the time to get a good photographer and made sure the weather and time of day was right. It enhanced the website and gives a professional finish.

When you're building a website, make sure you set aside time for the creative side of the project, as well as the setting up and functionality of the website."

Matt Poland

STOCK IMAGES
for your site

Stock photos are a fantastically useful resource. If you choose carefully, they don't have to look as though they're stock photos, and they're often surprisingly inexpensive; some platforms—Wix, Weebly, Squarespace, Strikingly—give you access to a built-in photo library right within their interface. There even plenty of free photographs available for use, if you know where to look. Here are some good sources:

http://www.shutterstock.com
http://www.istockphoto.com
https://fotolia.com
http://www.dreamstime.com
http://www.bigstockphoto.com

FREE RESOURCES

https://unsplash.com
https://pixabay.com
https://stocksnap.io
http://negativespace.co
https://picjumbo.com
http://deathtothestockphoto.com
http://www.gratisography.com
http://publicdomainarchive.com
https://images.google.com*

*Click on the cog at the right of your screen, choose "Advanced search" and select the"free to use or share, even commercially" option from the filter labeled "usage rights."

▷ You can easily find original photos for your website, that don't necessarily look like standard stock photos, at one of the independent, non-commercial stock photo libraries like Unsplash.
HTTPS://UNSPLASH.COM

CREDIT WHERE IT'S DUE

Be sure to credit the photographer and the source, if you need to. This will always be specified; if in doubt, ask. Don't save photos from other people's websites and use them on your own, without asking for permission—it's unethical, and illegal.

 CHECK THE PIXEL DIMENSIONS

When you're purchasing from a commercial stock library, make sure you buy an image that's bigger than you actually need it to be, then reduce it to the right size. Don't buy it too small, as you can't then make it bigger.

HEATHER CARSON
SELF-HOSTED WORDPRESS

| USA | HTTP://WWW.HEATHERCARSON.NET |

"Get clear on your branding first. What is the look and feel you want to create with your site? What is the purpose? This will determine what platform would be best, what template you pick, and the way you add your personal touches.

The platform you use will be less important than your content, so finding a platform that lets you easily create content is key.

If you're feeling overwhelmed with creating everything for your site, use pre-made design assets. You'll find clipart, stock photos, and many great online DIY graphic programs that are easy to use for all levels. For those without a big budget or a design background, you can use existing pieces to jump-start your website design."

Heather Carson

The TOOLS *you need*

You need two types of tool to work on the visuals for your site. The first is a tool you can use to crop and resize your photographs, as well as making small tweaks such as lightening them up. If you happen to have Photoshop, and know how to use it, that's brilliant, but you don't actually need anything anywhere near as sophisticated. My favorite alternative is the online tool Pixlr (https://pixlr.com; there's also a desktop version)—I'll show you the basics of how to use this tool below.

There are many others that will perform the same tasks for you; GIMP (https://www.gimp .org)—a desktop application for PC and Mac— and the online editors Fotor (http://www.fotor. com) and ON1 Perfect Photo Suite (http:// www.on1.com/apps/) are three of the best. Even the simple Apple Preview allows you to edit, crop, and resize photos, and this may be perfectly adequate for your needs (double click on the image to open it, then click the small toolbox icon to the right of the toolbar).

The second type of tool you'll need is one that can make graphics for your site that aren't just simple photographs—buttons, banners, etc. We'll look at some of these tools over the page.

WORKING WITH PIXLR

Go to https://pixlr.com/ and scroll down; choose the "Pixlr Editor" option. You don't have to sign up with them, but if you do, you can store images within the system. Now open the photo you want to edit. Suppose you want to resize and crop the photo shown in the screenshots so that it's a horizontal rectangle measuring 600×450 px, and you also want to lighten it up a bit so that the scenery is more visible.

1. First, resize the image so that it is 600 px wide. Click "Image size" from the "Image" menu in the Pixlr toolbar as shown.

2. Choose 600 for the width, keeping the "Constrain proportions" checkbox selected so that the picture isn't distorted. Click "OK".

3. The picture probably shows up rather small on your screen now so you can adjust the percentage to 80%—that way you can work with it more easily.

4. Now you need to crop the image. To do this, select the "Crop" tool from the toolbox on the left. Then choose "Output size" from the "Constraint" dropdown on the crop toolbar and type "600" and "450" into the "Width" and "Height" boxes. Click and drag your mouse over the photograph to mark out the shape, then click within the area to adjust the positioning so that the image looks good within the new rectangular shape. Press "Enter" to crop the image.

5. You now want to lighten it up a little. Choose "Brightness & Contrast" from the "Adjustment" menu. Adjust the sliders until you get the effect you want—here, increasing both the brightness and the contrast has made the background look more visible.

6. When your picture is as you want it, choose "File" >"Save" from the Pixlr menu. Rename the image if necessary and adjust the quality; as you can see here, reducing the quality by just 5% significantly reduces the file size. Save the image.

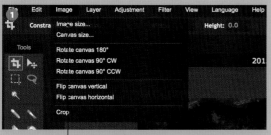

Click "Image size" to change the size

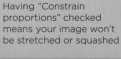

Having "Constrain proportions" checked means your image won't be stretched or squashed

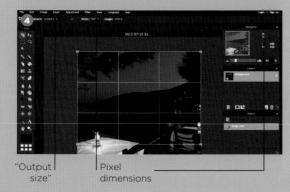

Make your image appear larger on the screen.

The Crop tool, found on the left-hand sidebar

"Output size"

Pixel dimensions

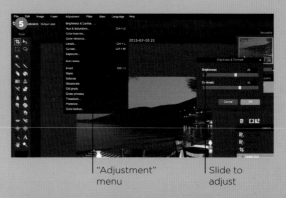

"Adjustment" menu

Slide to adjust

Pixlr can do pretty much anything you'd want it to do, as far as photo editing goes. If you need help, click on the "Help" button at the top right of the Pixlr menu bar; you can access tutorials and articles from here.

Adjust the quality here

The output file size

Tools to CREATE VISUALS

Creating graphics for your site is often a major challenge for the non-designer; it can make the difference between a site that's been professionally designed and one that's a DIY affair. But creating custom graphics doesn't have to be a stumbling block. Here are some easy-to-use tools that you can use to lift your site to that professional-looking level.

CANVA

Canva (https://www.canva.com) is the ultimate tool for the non-designer who wants to create great graphics. It allows you to create website graphics to pre-set dimensions—blog post graphics, infographics, Facebook "covers", rectangular ads, or other useful formats; or you can specify your own custom dimensions. You can even design matching printed materials such as postcards, gift certificates, and posters that you simply download ready for print.

What makes using Canva so much better than starting off with a blank canvas is that you can opt to kick off with a ready-designed template, which you then adjust according to your needs.

Above: **A beautiful photograph, carefully chosen and cropped, with writing added to it in an on-trend font, looks completely professional. You can achieve a look like this using Canva.**
HTTP://WWW.YOURHEALTHREVOLUTION.COM.AU

Below: **Colored social media buttons that tie in with the color scheme look much more individual than using the regular logos. Anyone can do this trick, and it looks great!**
HTTP://DESIGNLOVEFEST.COM

There's a whole library of icons and photos to use (many of which are free but the paid-for ones are entirely affordable) and you can also choose from a pre-curated selection of fonts and colors. You're more or less guaranteed to get something that looks amazing even if all you do is replace their text for yours and change the picture, but if you feel like playing around with shapes, filters, blur effects, backgrounds, and different fonts, you can let your creativity loose and come up with some really stunning and original graphics. And all of it without having to get involved with any expensive and complicated software.

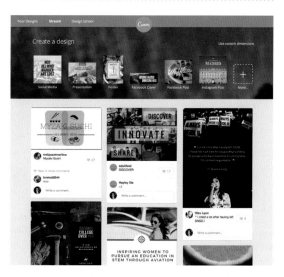

△ The Canva '"stream" shows the variety of graphics people are creating with the tool.

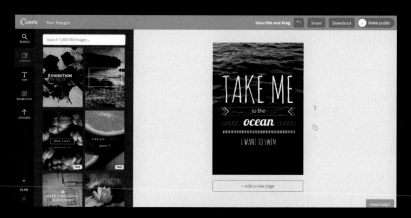

Left: With Canva you can start off with a ready-designed template which makes creating your own professional-looking graphics a breeze.

HTTPS:// WWW.CANVA.COM

Right: An easy and effective way of creating an interesting graphic that has more impact than a single simple photograph is by combining a number of photos using one of Canva's "grid" layouts and perhaps adding a "sticker" to it.

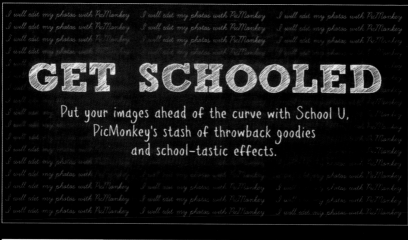

PicMonkey's "Themes" let you create graphics within a ready-defined "look," and their tutorials show you all kinds of tips and tricks to recreate the style of graphic you want.

HTTP://WWW.PICMONKEY.COM

PICMONKEY

PicMonkey (http://www.picmonkey.com is a photo editor as well as a graphics creator. With the "Royale" version (i.e. the paid-for version; you get a 30-day free trial), you can do most of what you'd want to do if you were a Photoshop expert, but much more easily and at a snip of the cost: fix blemishes, eliminate wrinkles, get rid of red-eye, remove shine, whiten teeth, add a tan... You can also create graphics for website headers or sliders and any other visuals, at custom sizes, that you want to put on your site, as well as photo collages to use on your blog.

Getting access to the premium tools costs around $3 a month if you go for the annual subscription—a really worthwhile investment if you produce a large number of website graphics. There aren't any pre-designed templates, though there are many "Themes" you can work with to achieve an on-trend look for your graphics (for example, the chalk-board look and super-hero comic book look, as shown above), and there are masses of tutorials. Many website owners opt for both Canva and the paid-for version of PicMonkey.

PIKTOCHART

Infographics are a way of communicating data that's far more engaging than just providing statistics, plus they're potentially "viral"—that is, if they look great and provide useful information, they tend to get spread about the web. Piktochart (http://piktochart.com) is one of the best online infographics makers available; it's easy to use and the free version offers you some great-looking templates, like the one shown below. (Also look at http://easel.ly, https://infogr.am, and http://visme.co; you can also make infographics using Canva.)

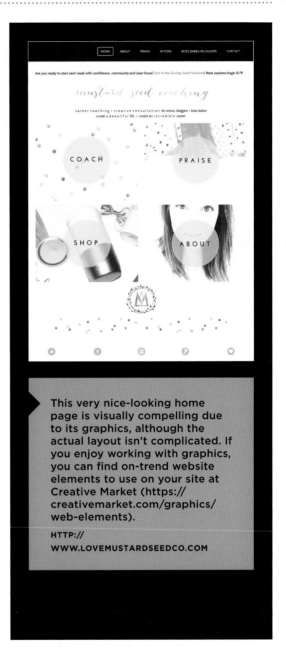

This very nice-looking home page is visually compelling due to its graphics, although the actual layout isn't complicated. If you enjoy working with graphics, you can find on-trend website elements to use on your site at Creative Market (https://creativemarket.com/graphics/web-elements).

HTTP://
WWW.LOVEMUSTARDSEEDCO.COM

△ It's easy to alter the Piktochart templates and create your own infographics, making information easily absorbable to your audience, and at the same time producing eminently "shareable" content.

HTTP://PIKTOCHART.COM

Some ideas for HORIZONTAL IMAGES

You'll have noticed that most website designs these days require a supply of images in a horizontal rectangular format—but it isn't always easy to find large-size horizontal images that fit into these spaces! Here are some ideas to help you conquer the horizontal image challenge.

1. Create a plain rectangle in a bold color and put lettering on it
If you need something very striking for a home page slider, why not go with the "flat design" trend and create a solid block of color and add a statement (or, if applicable, a date).

2. Use a pattern
Instead of solid color, use a wall-to-wall pattern (try http://thepatternlibrary.com, http://subtlepatterns.com, http://www.colourlovers.com/patterns, or https://creativemarket.com/graphics/patterns). (You may need to add a block of color, or a semi-transparent shape, behind any lettering you incorporate, so that it's legible.)

3. Fill the space with a solid color
The very simplest of ways of creating a wide horizontal image for your website is to fill up the necessary space next to your existing vertical image with a color, and perhaps add some wording in an interesting font.

4. Create a collage
Put several images together and create a rectangular graphic. Either Canva or PicMonkey will do the trick for you; you can add writing or a "sticker" to complete the graphic.

5. Create a collage that looks like separate images
Even though your template may only include space for a single wide image, you can compose an arrangement of individual elements (using Canva or Picmonkey) that look as though they are separate, and the design therefore more complex; the key is keeping the background the same color as the web page.

6. Create a collage using cutouts
Make a striking slider image by creating a hand-made collage, perhaps incorporating some cutouts. (You can cut out easily using Pixlr; choose the "Lasso" tool from the toolbar and use a "feather" of 5 pixels to make the cutout smoother. It's easiest if the item you want to cut out was photographed on a white background.)

7. Take photos with the format in mind
Perhaps the most obvious way of finding photos that fit into the horizontal format is to take suitable ones in the first place!

Right: **The easiest way to transform any photo into the required shape is to fill the gap with color.**

15 things to build with natural wood

DESIGN SHOW

Home   About   Blog   Contact

DESIGN SHOW
MARCH 20-23 2017

Left: **Use a solid block of colour if you need something striking but you don't have a photograph that will fit.**

Right: **Collages are perfect way for images that just don't work when cropped into the horizontal format; Canva offers every possible layout you could want for your collage.**

Left: **PicMonkey's "Cards" collage option is ideal for horizontal layouts. Once you've added your images, click the paint palette to adjust or change the color of the background.**

Left: **This nice-looking header is in fact a clever arrangement of elements within a single, wide image.**

WWW.COOKBOOK VILLAGE.COM
(Design: Wendy and Ruben Guerin)

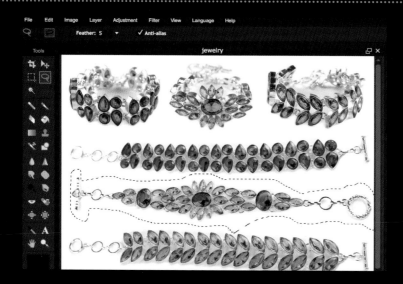

Left: **Cutout collages create a more individual and magazine-like look; try adding writing into the collage. Seen here, cutting out an object with a white background using Pixlr.**

Right: **Seen here, a cut-out collage with writing added to it, created to fill a horizontal space.**

HTTP://
WWW.THEWHITEPEPPER.COM

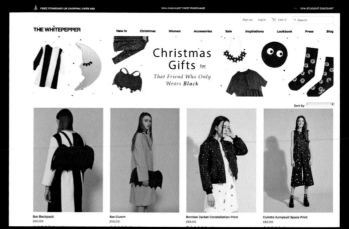

Left: **Patterns can make striking, modern backgrounds for banners. Used here, "Science" by Fabricio Marques at The Pattern Library.**

HTTP://THEPATTERNLIBRARY.COM

YUCHING CHEN PORTFOLIO
STRIKINGLY

USA

HTTP://WWW.RACCOONFLY.COM

"As an artist, I want to impress the audience with my work, but I also need to be able to maintain my website easily without any hassle. Strikingly is a very easy, hands-on tool. It is simple to learn and use and I can modify the content at any time with a few clicks. It's a great way for people to build their first website.

Browsing the internet inspired me how to design my own website. It helped me to work out the layout and I got inspiration from various kinds of styles. But of course, your own images and text are the most important elements."

Yuching Chen

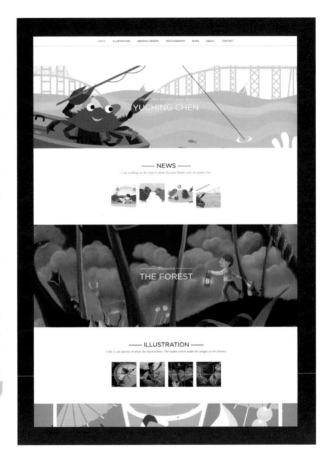

Your LOGO

Even if you're not a company, your website needs a logo. Don't worry, it doesn't need to look corporate if that isn't appropriate—at its very simplest, it can simply be your name, or the name of the website, written in a suitable font.

You can either create your own logo, or get a professional to do it for you. Obviously, the ideal solution is to use a skilled professional; they'll ask you questions about your target audience, create a mood board, and so on, and ultimately create something that suits your purposes ideally. Worry not if this is out of the question—you can easily create something yourself that is perhaps not entirely unique, but will happily fulfill its function in a way that's appropriate, and is also pleasing to the eye.

CREATING YOUR LOGO YOURSELF

Use an online logo generator
Today there are some really good online logo makers available. If you're in doubt as to your design skills, pick a very, very simple design—and of course, do some canvassing amongst both trusted advisers and members of your target audience.

Some places you can create a logo online are:

http://www.squarespace.com/logo/—A very simple, but effective, generator offered by the makers of Squarespace (whether or not you're using their platform—there's a small fee for the printable version if not), based on icons.

https://withoomph.com—Not free, but a good, and very easy way to create a simple logo; you can also generate a printable version.

http://hipsterlogogenerator.com—This is only suitable for a precise style of logo, the badge-style retro look. But if this is the style of your website, you may have found your answer.

Do beware—there are numerous other online generators available, but they do tend to look cheap or generic.

Use lettering for your logo
This is a very easy way of creating a logo, and you can even create something striking and memorable this way—but you do need to choose the right font! You can get interesting fonts at http://www.fontsquirrel.com (free) or https://creativemarket.com/fonts (premium, but relatively low-cost); install them on your computer and access via Pixlr.

Get a logo designed
If you want to get a logo designed but your budget is limited, try http://99designs.com or for an extremely inexpensive option https://www.fiverr.com.

It's also worth knowing about the 99Designs "Tasks" service (https://en.99designs.fr/tasks/). It's a fabulous place to find designers who can create logos, brochures, business cards, ebook layouts, website visuals and any other graphic material you might need, at extremely reasonable prices.

DAN CARR PHOTOGRAPHY
SELF-HOSTED WORDPRESS

| CANADA | HTTP://DANCARRPHOTOGRAPHY.COM |

"My website has always been a hugely important part of my business and I know that when I email potential clients, the first thing they probably do is click my website link from the footer of my email.

I make sure that the first impression they get is one that underlines my experience, the quality of my work and my past clients. This opens the door to an ongoing conversation.

My site is my number one marketing tool so I make sure I check in with it every day to answer comments, check for plugin updates and make sure everything is working as it should.

The key factor for me was the sheer amount of information on the web about WordPress. If you don't mind sifting through it all, you can find the answer to nearly every query. Calling Divi* a "theme" doesn't really do it justice though because it's more like a framework. You can customize the basic layout of Divi pretty easily, so you could make two sites from it that nobody would ever guess are based on the same theme."

Dan Carr

*See page 105

7 Video & Audio

△ Kendra Valentine's award-winning website Americulinariska is a great example of how to use video for hands-on cookery demonstrations.

HTTP://WWW.AMERICULINARISKA.COM

Video adds life to your website in a way that photos and words just can't. Video is so easy to make these days and so easy to put on your website that it makes sense to join in with this growing trend—and growing it is, with Cisco predicting that by 2019, consumer internet video traffic will be 80% of all consumer internet traffic!

There are two main reasons why you might want to incorporate audio into your site. The first is that you're a musician, or perhaps a stand-up comedian or spoken word poet, and you want your site visitors to access your audio (rather than video) straight from your site. Or secondly, you might want to start a podcast; just as with video, it's really easy to include audio in your website.

IDEAS FOR VIDEO *on your site*

- An introduction on the home page, welcoming visitors and presenting the website or the business. You can use the style of the video to communicate your brand style or the "lifestyle" into which the site visitors are "buying."
- On your "About" page, to bring you or the business to life. You could show the various members of staff at work, or show the viewer around the premises. You could give a more in-depth view of yourself, what you do, what you like, your influences and yourself at work (for artists), yourself playing (for musicians), your studio, a tour around your exhibition or your show, etc.
- How-to videos. This could be explaining how to use or set up one of your products (this could go on your "FAQ" page and help to cut down on customer service queries.) Or, if your website's chief purpose is to provide information, you could create "how-to" videos as a core part of your website content, which keeps visitors coming back to your site—many people prefer to watch a demonstration rather than read a tutorial.

- Use videos as testimonials. A happy client speaking into the camera makes a much more convincing testimonial than simply publishing their words.
- Show your products in use, and announce new products. (Apparently 64% of consumers are more likely to buy a product after watching a video about it—a figure provided by comScore, http://www.comscore.com.)
- Show recent events and activities at your business.
- Video blogging ("vlogging"). Some bloggers choose to make a video that is like a mini TV episode and post it as a blog post, with either a transcript, or introductory text, to accompany it.

Pico De Gallo Salsa | Americulinariska

2:39 / 3:33

◁ Practical demonstrations will keep people coming back to your website. Cookery may be an ideal subject for video, but it could be used for anything you can make or do.

HTTP://WWW.
AMERICULINARISKA.COM

INCORPORATING VIDEO *into your site*

No matter which platform you're using, you'll find it easy to display video on your site. You first have to upload your video to a video streaming service like YouTube or Vimeo (making sure it is not set to "Private," which would, of course, prevent your site visitors from viewing it).

Then, depending on the platform, you'll either add the URL of the video directly into the page into a video element or block, depending on how your platform works. Or you'll copy and paste the "embed code" of the video into an area of your admin where you can insert website code. There's nothing complicated—you just have to copy and paste; your platform will give you precise instructions.

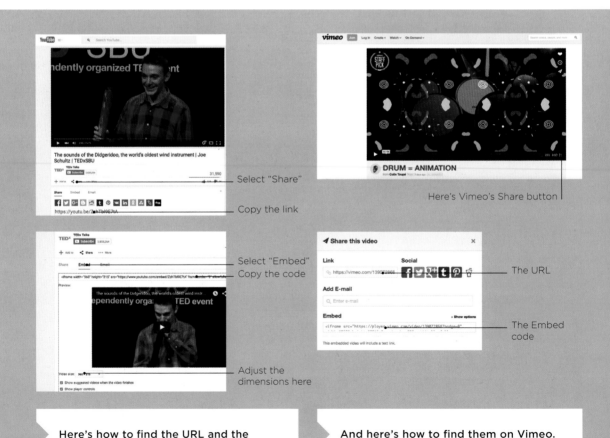

Select "Share"

Copy the link

Here's Vimeo's Share button

Select "Embed"
Copy the code

The URL

The Embed code

Adjust the dimensions here

Here's how to find the URL and the embed code of a video on YouTube.

And here's how to find them on Vimeo.

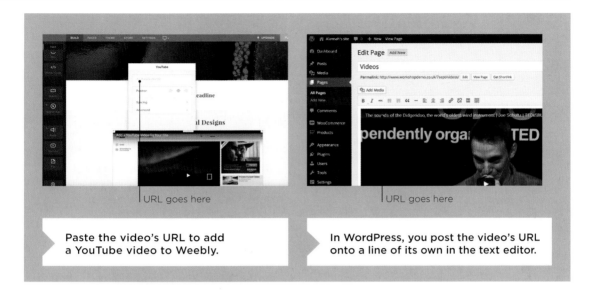

URL goes here

URL goes here

> **Paste the video's URL to add a YouTube video to Weebly.**

> **In WordPress, you post the video's URL onto a line of its own in the text editor.**

YOUTUBE OR VIMEO?

YouTube (https://www.youtube.com) is the larger platform and you can grow a massive following or have your video go viral. Search engine optimization is built-in, and YouTube is owned by Google, which means that its videos get listed highly. Vimeo (https://vimeo.com), on the other hand, looks smarter, has more customization possibilities, and is a more eclectic community; it's up to you to see which one suits your profile, and your aims, best.

OTHER EMBEDS

You're not restricted to just videos hosted on YouTube and Vimeo. Your platform should allow you to incorporate video published in many other places (CNN, Dailymotion, Forbes, National Geographic, Vine, etc.) simply by adding the URL—if not, you'll be able to use their embed code by pasting it into an area in which you can paste HTML.

PERISCOPE

The Periscope app (https://www.periscope.tv; iOS and Android) is a fantastic way of broadcasting live to your circle (or anyone else who's curious and happens to stumble upon you). While you can't replay a Periscope video more than 24 hours after it was made (and that's only if you choose to set it that way), you can save it and repurpose it to YouTube, and then publish it on your website.

VIDEO GALLERIES

If you have a lot of videos to include on your site—for example, if you're a musician—you'll probably want to group your videos into a gallery so they're displayed in a neater, more professional way. WordPress and Squarespace have a built-in gallery feature for videos; other platforms have apps that allow you this kind of display. (I've also listed a useful tool for grouping videos on page 163.)

MAKING *your own* VIDEOS

Just as with photographs, a professionally made video will look much more polished than one you've made yourself, but the good news is that perfectly acceptable videos for your website can be produced with little more than an iPhone, or other smartphone (for a simple "talking head" you can just use your computer's camera). The following tips will help you:

- Lighting is essential. As with photography, natural light is the best, but if you don't have a strong enough light source, surround the area you want to film (or yourself!) with multiple light sources.
- Use a tripod.
- Don't zoom in with your phone's camera—you'll lose quality. It's much better to move the camera closer.
- Reduce background noise as much as you can. Turn off music (you can add in music later if you want), fans, and humming fridges, and close windows.
- Using an external microphone, even a small clip-on lapel microphone, will help you achieve better sound quality. (Or, you can use another phone and record onto a dedicated voice-recording app; you then remove the original audio from the video, and add the new one).
- Consider the background. You may wish to be seen talking at your desk, for example, in a natural way, but check what the viewers will be able to see—watch out for electric sockets and radiators, for example, which seem to look much more visible when they're on camera. Similarly, if you're using a "fake" white or patterned background, make sure your viewers can't see the edges.

- Write a script. You may want your video to sound as though you're speaking "off the cuff," but preparing a script, even if you're not intending to read from it, is a good way to get clear about what you're going to say and how you're going to say it, before you start to speak.
- Include your logo and website address at the end. If it's a promotional video, also include a call to action: "Sign up," "Visit our website at... to order," etc.
- It's usually best to keep the video short, unless you're creating a detailed how-to or longer interview. For interviews, you may want to consider cutting the video into shorter, separate sections that will keep the viewer engaged more easily.
- You don't need any very fancy editing software—you can use iMovie, or any simple editor like Windows Movie Maker.
- Simple transitions (how you move from one shot to another) usually look much better than trying your hand with fancy ones.
- Consider adding music at the beginning and the end—it adds a professional touch. (You can get inexpensive music clips from stock libraries.)
- As well as posting your video on your website or blog, share it on social media.

INCORPORATING AUDIO *into your site*

Most platforms give you a choice of whether you want to include the audio track just as it is, or as a SoundCloud embed. (Some platforms, such as Strikingly, will only let you include a SoundCloud embed rather than letting you upload the audio track to your website.)

SoundCloud is basically the YouTube of audio. Whether you want to include the audio track just as it is, or the SoundCloud embed, depends on whether you want your audio to have the added visibility of being present on a hugely

popular platform, or whether your audio is essentially just for your site visitors. There's also the look of it to consider—a plain audio "player" looks quite sober, whereas a SoundCloud embed has the added visual element and can look more lively or modern.

You can also embed whole SoundCloud playlists to your site. Exactly as with embedding videos, you may be asked to embed either the SoundCloud URL, or the "embed code," depending on your platform.

Inserting an audio block with Squarespace.

Embedding a SoundCloud clip with Strikingly.

SoundCloud embed

Uploaded track

A SoundCloud embed and an uploaded track shown on a WordPress site; note that there are dozens of WordPress plugins that allow you to display audio in different ways.

RECORDING *audio*

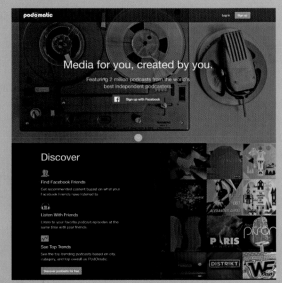

Bandcamp lets you set up a page for your band from where fans can purchase and download tracks and albums.
HTTPS://CONVEYOR.BANDCAMP.COM

PodOmatic is one of a number of all-in-one services that host your podcast for you.
HTTPS://PODOMATIC.COM

- Prepare thoroughly and script what you're going to say unless you're absolutely confident you can ad lib without stumbling.
- An external microphone will give you better sound than just recording onto your computer.
- You don't need fancy recording or editing software—try Audacity (http://audacityteam .org) or GarageBand (http://www.apple. com/mac/garageband/)
- Record in as quiet a place as you possibly can, to cut down on background noise.
- Use a 128K Constant Bit Rate and export your files in MP3 format.

- For a podcast, as with video, overlaying music at the beginning and at the end makes it really sound like a professional radio program.
- To record a Skype conversation (for example if you're conducting an interview for a podcast), try Call Recorder for Skype (http://www.ecamm.com/mac/ callrecorder/) or Audio Hijack (https:// rogueamoeba.com/audiohijack/) for Mac, or MP3 Skype Recorder (http:// voipcallrecording.com) or Pamela (http:// www.pamela.biz) for PC.

PODCASTING

A podcast is like having your own radio station, with new listeners stumbling upon you and getting to know you and your work via your program. You can't podcast from every type of website as you need a blog feed to enable your podcast to work as it's meant to—that is, downloading automatically to reach listeners as you release new episodes. Squarespace or WordPress sites (either .com or the self-hosted version) are ideal. This is what you need to do:

1. First record your audio.

2. Upload it to your website. Embed your audio file into a post (WordPress) or as an audio block into a blog post (Squarespace; within the "Podcasting" tab of the audio block editing area, you can give precise details about the specific episode, add keywords and the audio duration).

3. For self-hosted WordPress, you'll need a free plugin such as Blubrry PowerPress (which you can install directly from your WordPress admin area).

   Create your cover art in a square format, minimum size 1400x1400 px. For WordPress, upload this image to your media library, copy the image URL (click on the image and look on the right-hand side of the window to find the URL), and paste it into the required field in the PowerPress area of your admin. Fill out the other fields too: summary, iTunes category, etc.

   For Squarespace, you need to enable iTunes RSS tags. This you do inside the blog page settings, within the Syndication tab; there are precise instructions inside the support area if you can't see where this is. Scroll down to the bottom of this same area and upload your cover art, and complete the other boxes as well.

For WordPress.com, create a category for your blog posts (e.g. Podcasts) and assign the blog post you've just created with the audio file embedded into it, to that category. Then go to "Settings" > "Media" and under the "Podcasting" section, fill in the required information.

4. Copy your "RSS feed" and submit it to iTunes. To do this, follow the link on this web page, step 5: http://www.apple.com/itunes/podcasts/specs.html. (Alternatively, go to the iTunes Store, click Podcasts, then "Submit a podcast" from the right-hand menu—it takes you to the same place.)

5. Wait for confirmation that your podcast has been accepted by iTunes. This can take some days.

PODCASTING SERVICES

Rather than hosting your podcast yourself, it may be more practical to use an all-in-one service like PodOmatic to record, broadcast, store your audio files, and submit your RSS feed to iTunes; this will enable you to podcast whatever website building platform you're using. (https://www.podomatic.com)

8

Blogging

You may be creating your website specifically because you want to blog, in which case you're already sold on the joys of blogging— getting your voice heard and entering into a community of like-minded others all over the world, who are passionate about the same things as you.

But what might not have occurred to you, if you're setting up a business website, is that it a blog could be a valuable addition to your new website—whether you sell products or professional services, or your site is a showcase for your talents or artworks.

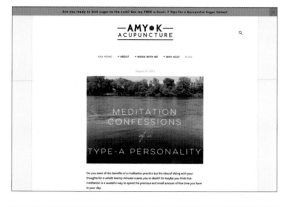

▷ **Two blogs for service business websites: acupuncture and counseling. Blogging about and around a subject gives a business a friendly, human face.**
HTTP://WWW.AMYKACU.COM Design: Kimberly Boustead
HTTP://WWW.BWCSONLINECOUNSELING.COM Design/ development: http://www.bddcreatives.com

WHY ADD A BLOG
to your website?

Every kind of website will benefit from the addition of a well-done blog. Read on for some of the compelling reasons why setting up a blog, even if your website is primarily a business website, is such a sensible thing to do, and why you might really be missing out if you choose not to.

- If you want to make the most of social media to promote your website—and you're turning your back on a massive opportunity if you don't—you need something to share that isn't simply other people's content. People don't usually share regular website pages, or product pages, but they do share useful and interesting material posted on a blog— provided of course, that it's really useful and interesting enough; this alone could be your primary motivation for starting a blog, but there are other reasons, too.
- Google likes relevant content on a website. If your site has just a few pages, it won't carry much weight with Google. But if you have a blog on your site, you now have quantities of content that relates directly to your subject matter. This is another huge reason for setting up a blog.
- Google also likes sites that are updated often (which blogs should be—if you can't do it often, at least do it regularly).
- Having more "Googleable" content ultimately means more people will find you, which gives you the opportunity to connect and share with more people and enlarge your reach.
- A blog is a way of standing out. If you show that you understand your customers' problems and offer some realistic solutions, the chances are that the customer will come to you, over someone else who doesn't appeal to them directly.
- Your blog can reinforce your unique selling point, your values, your philosophy. (Or, if you're not selling, what it is that makes you different from everyone else in the same field as you.)
- It creates an image of you or the business that the rest of the website can't do—not even the "About" page, however interesting you make it. It can engage readers on a human level. It gives them a taste of you—your style, and what it would be like to be talking, working, or doing business with you.
- If you're selling a lifestyle, it's the perfect opportunity to "flesh out" what that lifestyle is.
- Recent, regular posts on a blog makes you look modern and up-to-date. It gives a clear signal that you are alive, active, and available.
- It also makes you pretty much impossible to copy. If your blog shows plenty of personality, no one else's can be the same. (A business site, even for a serious service, can show personality.)
- Finally, it's nice to share. Giving people some of your basic expertise costs you nothing and provides an opportunity to help and connect with others.

Some tips for BLOGGING SUCCESS

There really are no hard-and-fast rules when it comes to blogging, but there definitely are certain things that will help you. Many of these are just the same as for website-building in general: people like attractive graphics, a friendly, uncluttered layout, and will be drawn in by an attention-grabbing headline. Blog posts are also a very good way to share content on social media and connect with a vast audience of potential clients, customers, contributors, etc., and so it's worth thinking about how you'll maximize your shareability when creating blog posts. Here are some tips to help you get started:

Plan your blog posts ahead of time

It's important to be regular with your blog posts to show your readers that you're still alive and in business. You don't have to post more than once a week, or even once a month if it suits you better. Just be regular—there's little more discouraging than to see an abandoned blog on a website. Create an editorial calendar ahead of time, and even prepare your blog posts in advance, to ensure you can do this.

Add visuals to your blog posts

Not only do visuals make your posts look more inviting, but they also get shared on social media. Use Canva and an easy-to-use tool such as Pablo (which creates graphics out of words; https://buffer.com/pablo) to create "shareable" graphics that you put into your posts.

Remember who you're writing for

When you're writing, remember you're not writing to impress your peers (unless, of course, this actually is the point of your blog!) Most people will either be writing for for like-minded people who share the same interest, or their potential customers or clients. So, address their needs, talk to them, share. Don't show off, or speak in jargon that alienates them.

How long should a blog post be?

There's a lot of discussion and analysis around how long the ideal blog post should be. Some people say 600 words, others have come up with the ideal figure of 1,600—but really, you can make your blog post just as long as you want it to be. The real point is quality.

Vary your content

Keep your blog lively by writing different kinds of post and including video from time to time, even if yours isn't a video blog, just to keep your audience entertained. (See overleaf for some ideas for blog posts.)

Guest posting

Guest posting is when you invite someone to write a post for your blog, or they agree to let you write on theirs. It's a very good way of coming into contact with a slightly different audience—and of offering your own audience something different.

Think about the search engines

If sharing your valuable content and attracting traffic via the search engines was one of your major motivations for starting a blog on your site, you need to think about each blog post with the search engines in mind. Do some keyword research and craft the title and the

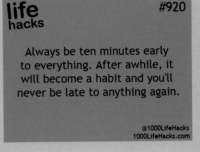

life hacks #920

Always be ten minutes early to everything. After awhile, it will become a habit and you'll never be late to anything again.

@1000LifeHacks
1000LifeHacks.com

◁◁ Creating graphics for you blog posts means that people can share them; create graphics out of words, if your content doesn't lend itself to images—as with the "life hacks" example (above).
HTTP://1000LIFEHACKS.COM
HTTP://
WWW.MAKINGHOMEBASE.COM

blog post content around the keywords or phrases you want to target (see Chapter 11), or a specific question or problem you know your readers have. It's important you include the right words, in order for your post to be found and read by the people you want to read it.

Pay attention to your headlines

Think about your blog post titles. These will either make a reader click to read the post, or not click! Jot down a few for each blog post and pick the best—the others you can use later, to vary the way you introduce that blog post on the different social media.

Keep your voice authentic

The tone of your blog will depend on what you are writing about and how familiar you want to be with your readers. Whatever tone you decide is suitable for your audience, whether you want to sound super-friendly or a bit more professional, your voice will need to sound authentic. One way of doing this is to pick the person you are addressing and write with them in mind—maybe imagining a close friend, or a client; this can help you sound real.

Make a checklist

Before you post to your blog, check spelling and grammar, check the title, check you've optimized for the search engines, check any links, credit any images. And after you post, check again, make graphics you can use to add to your social media posts (see Chapter 10), and check for comments. Make yourself a checklist to keep yourself on track!

Blog
INSPIRATION

△ Elizabeth Minchilli's beautiful Rome-based blog.
△ HTTP://WWW.ELIZABETHMINCHILLIINROME.COM
Design: Nicolee Drake

△ Cool travel spot curation blog Melting Butter.
HTTP://WWW.MELTINGBUTTER.COM Design: Veronique
De Koning, http://www.veroniquedekoning.nl

△ Collaborative editorial blog It Ain't Necessarily So.
◁ HTTP://WWW.ITAINTNECESSARILYSO.ORG Design:
Nichole Fernandez

◁ Stacy Millican's eclectic book blog.
HTTP://WWW.THENOVELLIFE.COM

Some Ideas for Blog Posts

If you're setting up a website specifically to blog, you're probably brimming with ideas of blog posts you want to write. For days when you're short of an idea— or if you're following my advice and setting up a blog as part of your business website, and perhaps aren't quite certain where to start—take a look at this list for some inspiration:

- How-to articles or tutorials—these are amazingly popular and of real value to your readers.
- Product reviews and comparisons are frequently Googled-for so they're great for expanding your reach.
- Behind-the-scenes photos and stories.
- Stories of how products, creations, or works of art came into being.
- Inspirational stories.
- Recounting an incident that brought you an insight that you can share with your readers.
- Stories that illustrate the usefulness of your products.
- Clients' success stories.
- Top ten (or any other number) tips.
- Top ten tools.
- Top ten tricks.
- Top ten reasons.
- Top ten best ideas.
- Best resources.
- A curated list of links to other people's articles on a particular topic.
- In-the-know-information that positions you as an expert.
- Industry updates.
- Trends.
- Interviews with other people.
- Recorded Skype interviews.

- Best wins of last year.
- Aims for the coming year.
- What have you seen in the past week that has inspired you?
- What surprising facts have you come across in your field during the last week?
- Asking opinions and getting feedback from readers, surveys, polls.
- Quizzes.
- Competitions—write in to win, or share on social media.
- Checklists.
- Posts featuring photos sent in by readers using or wearing your products.
- Share your favorite websites or blogs.
- Create a series—thereby creating anticipation for the coming posts.
- The most common myths about...
- Recount your professional successes and failures.
- Solutions to problems you know your readership experiences (people may have emailed you about them).
- Readers' questions answered.
- What you wished you knew when you began doing what you do now.
- Anything that you know will fascinate your readers, that they will want to share on social media.

9 Email *Newsletters*

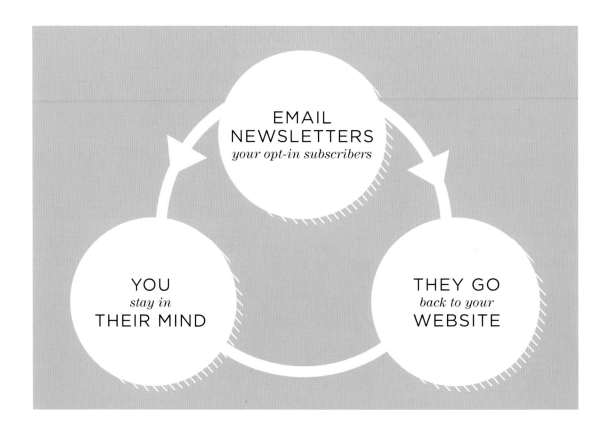

Publishing on your blog is brilliant, but it depends on people coming back to your site. What happens if they forget all about you and never come back? How are you supposed to stay in their minds that way? That's why it makes sense to get their email address and contact them by email. They already spend time on email every day and they'll certainly see it if your newsletter pops into their inbox. We are not talking about spamming them here, of course. We are talking about sending them emails with their permission; this kind of emailing is called "opt-in," because the individuals have chosen to be on your list.

The importance of NEWSLETTERS & why they WORK

The goal of your newsletter is probably two-fold:

1. To stay in people's minds.
2. To send them back to your website where they can purchase, hire you, or further explore your free content and experience the benefit of your knowledge and the unique vision of your brand.

The important thing to realize about your email list is that it is not the number of people you have on your list that make it successful, but the relationship you have with those people.

So, it could be that you have a small list of a hundred people, but if those people are loyal supporters of yours and turn up to every show (for example), and bring their friends who also absolutely want to buy your work, then your email list is a wonderful asset to you even if it is small. Conversely, if you have a large list but those people don't know you, or care about you or what you're offering, then you're not going to get good results if you invite them to your next show and ask them to bring their friends, or suggest that they buy your work online.

So, in essence, your email list is a way to develop your relationship with your fan base, whatever it is that you do.

What do you mail out to your subscribers? It's entirely up to you. Some people send out just a few words when they have an announcement to make, others send regular, full-blown newsletters to their subscribers complete with tips, resources, updates, and articles. Often, an email may simply include a little bit of chatty text plus a link to your most recent blog post, and that's usually quite enough. Remember that people are busy—not everyone has the time to read a full newsletter—so unless you actually want to create a proper newsletter, a short email will usually work just as well. As long as it is interesting enough for your subscribers to want to read it, then you'll have achieved your goals.

How often you contact your subscribers is also your own decision, and what is appropriate depends also on your field. But the key is staying in their minds and establishing a "friendship" with them, so that if they need what you are offering, be it information, products, or your services, you're the obvious choice to go to.

YOUR FREE GIVEAWAY

The typical way of encouraging people to sign up is by giving away something for free in return for their email address. You need to make sure you give them something that's really good, as it's the only flavor they've had up until now of what interaction with you is like, and will pave the way for the future. A free download (in pdf format) is the most common option, but everyone does this. Think how you can stand out from the crowd—the idea is to ensure it's such amazing quality, or so original, or so useful, that they can't wait to get more from you!

Alternative offerings could be free tickets, discount coupons, an audio download, a video, checklist, email course (delivered by autoresponder—automatic email—which can be provided by your mailing list manager), webinar, printable workbook, recipes, paper patterns—even a free consultation, if you have the time. You can be as creative as you like in dreaming up something that's really going to encourage your potential subscribers to sign up, and please them when they have.

EMAIL LIST MANAGERS

Obviously, you need a proper email list manager to take care of your list and mail your newsletters out, whether or not you choose a structured newsletter format or a more informal personal email-style message.

Some of the most popular email list managers are:

MailChimp http://mailchimp.com
AWeber http://www.aweber.com
Mad Mimi (https://madmimi.com)
iContact (https://www.icontact.com)
Constant Contact (http://www.constantcontact.com)

MailChimp is often used by starting-out entrepreneurs as they offer a free service for up to 2,000 subscribers. For this reason we'll take MailChimp as an example and look at how it's set up, but the other services offer a very high quality service as well. Note that the free account with MailChimp doesn't include an autoresponder feature (automatic email delivery that's used for email courses); this is only available for premium accounts.

YOUR SIGNUP FORM

Your email list provider will give you the code for a signup form which you can either into your site, or use an app or a widget. You want to put your signup form in multiple different places on your website. Good places are in a bar at the top of each page (you can install a bar like this using SumoMe; see page 161), in the sidebar (side column) of your site, and at the bottom of each page or blog post if your system allows (for self-hosted WordPress, you can use Popup Ally for this—page 167); popups are also vastly effective (again, see SumoMe). You may need to play around with the positioning of your signup forms, and the wording you put on them, in order to maximize your signup rate.

Newsletter IDEAS

See what other people are doing in your niche, and think what you can do to stand out from the others, yet still communicate effectively in a way that your subscribers will appreciate. For example, you could decide to include videos if others aren't doing that (the way to do this is to include a screenshot of the video as an image in the email, and link to it on YouTube, or wherever it is hosted) just to make it a bit different. Certainly include images, if only a couple—they make the email so much more appealing, plus readers are interested to see shots of you at work, and other behind the scenes stuff that perhaps only subscribers get treated to.

Here are some ideas for newsletter content for your newsletter:

- Monthly tip (or however often it is that you publish).
- Readers' Q&A.
- FAQ.
- Videos.
- Links to the latest blog posts on your website, plus introductory text.
- Introducing your latest products.
- Announce social media competitions (or other competitions).
- Give discount codes for subscribers.
- Exclusive offers.
- Pictures of you at events, sales, or even a sneak peek of yourself away on holiday, perhaps doing something unusual.
- Behind-the-scenes images.
- Company updates and news (keep these customer-centric if possible).
- Seasonal tips or other relevant content.
- Surveys or polls.
- Survey and poll results.
- Customer testimonials.
- Case studies.
- Press mentions and awards.
- Industry news—but only if it applies to the readers (and not only to your peers).
- "Save the dates" for the future.
- Local news—if applicable.
- Tools and resources you've come across plus your personal opinion on them.
- Introduce other people, perhaps causes you're supporting, or others in complementary areas of interest.
- Books you're reading—relevant to your topic.
- Staff favorites (among your products, if applicable).
- Inspirational quotations.
- Ask your readers for feedback—is there anything they would like to hear about from you?

Again—you don't need to spend a huge amount of time on your newsletter, if you don't want to. Just a quick email with a link to your blog post plus an explanation or introduction can be perfectly adequate to keep you in the mind of your readers and encourage them to click over to your website.

SETTING UP *MailChimp*

Sign up from the home page, and click the activation button in your email. You'll be required to supply some information, such as your address—this is to conform to the regulations (as explained further in Chapter 14). I recommend you opt in to receive

MailChimp's "Getting Started" series of emails about how the system works—it is, actually, fairly complex, simply because it's very full-featured. There's also an online guide that you can access at the bottom of the first screen that you get taken to.

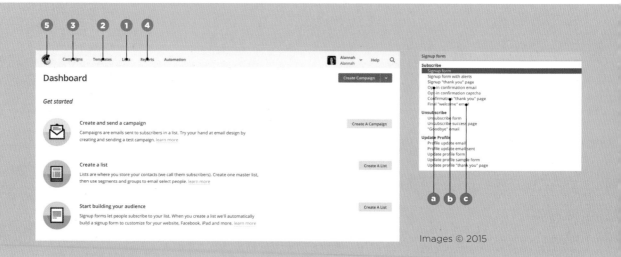

Images © 2015

The system offers you a quick-start series of buttons on the admin home page.

1. Create your list here. You can add subscribers individually, or import a previously existing list, or import from Google Contacts or any CRM (customer relationship management) software you may already use, such as Highrise.

    Here is also where you create signup forms and the emails that your subscribers receive when they sign up; click on the name of the list, and then on "Signup forms." "Embedded forms" are what you want for your website; create the form as you want it, and then copy the code. Your

platform will allow you to paste in a code element, or they may have an app that is easier to use. You can also create a popup form here, but this is fairly complicated— you'll almost certainly find it more straightforward to use a tool like SumoMe instead—obviously you'll connect it with your MailChimp account—and skip using the MailChimp popup.

You may also want to change the wording of emails that people receive when they sign up to your list, to make it seem more personal. Go to "General Forms" within the "Signup forms" area area. Then from the dropdown labeled "Forms and response emails" select and make adjustments to the following emails: Opt-in confirmation email (a), Confirmation "thank-you" page (b), and Final "welcome" email (c). For the final "welcome" email, you'll need to check the checkbox confirming you'd like your subscribers to receive this, and then, if you're giving them access to a download, this is where you'll include the download link. Mouse over the area where it says, "Your subscription to our list has been confirmed" and then click on the "Edit" button. Change the text as you wish, click on the link icon, choose "File" and upload your file to MailChimp; click "Insert" then "Save & Close."

You probably won't need to configure the other emails or web pages, nor the signup web page itself, as you'll most likely be including a signup form on your website. If you're finding this a bit too complex, you can safely leave all the settings just as they are, although you will need to configure the final "welcome" email if you want to include a free download link as above.

2. Create a template here. This is only necessary if you want your emails to look like a properly formatted newsletter—if you only want to send an informal-looking email, you don't need to do this. However, it's actually quite easy, and fun, to create a nice-looking template using the simple drag-and-drop interface, so don't be put off by the more complicated Step 1.

3. When you're ready to send out an email, click "Campaigns," and then "Create a Campaign." (A "campaign" is simply MailChimp-speak for sending out a mailing.) Choose between a newsletter format email, an informal text email, and an "RSS feed" email—this is an email that includes your recent blog posts, and is sent out automatically when there are new blog posts available, as often as you decide. (If you need help locating the web address for your "feed," ask your platform for assistance.) Follow the steps throughout the procedure; use the tabs at the top to preview your mailing, and be sure to run a test email that you can check thoroughly before sending for real. When you're ready, click "Send."

4. Here's where you check your reports, following each mailing—this will include details about how many people opened it, which links they clicked in the email, etc.

5. Return to the Dashboard by clicking the monkey. After you've sent out your first campaign, your Dashboard will show the stats of your recent campaigns and signups.

EMAILING WITHIN THE LAW

You need to stick to some precise rules when mailing out to your opt-in list. These aren't too hard to comply with and many are set in place in any case by your mailing list provider; see Chapter 14 for details.

NEWSLETTER FORMAT OR PLAIN TEXT?

You may want to reinforce your branding, in which case a newsletter format will probably be your choice, or you may see it as more important to try and strike a more informal tone with your readers.

10 *Social* Media

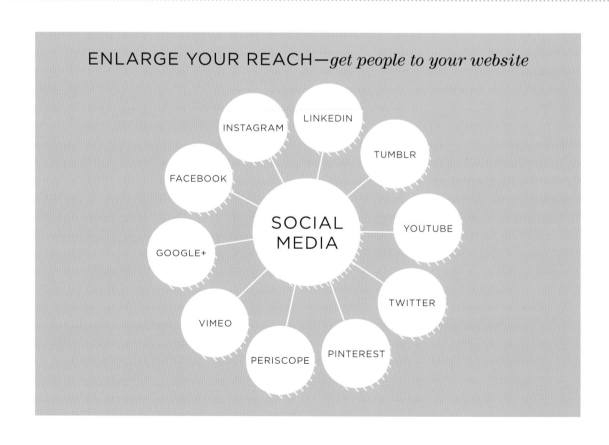

ENLARGE YOUR REACH—*get people to your website*

SOCIAL MEDIA

- INSTAGRAM
- LINKEDIN
- TUMBLR
- FACEBOOK
- YOUTUBE
- GOOGLE+
- TWITTER
- VIMEO
- PERISCOPE
- PINTEREST

Social media as a PROMOTIONAL TOOL

Using social media to promote your website is something you definitely want to do. Getting other people to share your content is free marketing—potentially on a gigantic scale, and to people all over the world.

Trends come and go, new systems appear, and the different platforms all function in slightly different ways, but let's consider social media as a whole here, to get a global view of its overall role.

Social media works broadly like this: you use one of the platforms to publish content of yours—whether in the form of a post, a tweet, a video, a pin, and so—and if the people who come into contact with what you published appreciate it, they will "share" it to their network so their connections also see it: this next level of people may, in turn, choose to pass it on, if they like it enough. This way, you get to "harness" the power of an amazing machine that works simply by the power of people liking what you've shown them, and the spread can potentially be massive.

In this chapter we're talking specifically about how social media can be used to promote your website. So when you're using social media for promotional ends, rather than just having fun and sharing things you like with your circle, you're actually concentrating on two main aims:

1. To extend your reach, and increase your "know, like, and trust"* factor.
2. To encourage people to click back to your website, where they can read your content, sign up for your newsletter, follow your blog, make purchases, or hire you.

This is where your blog—or other website content—comes in. When you have your own content, you have something that people can share and that will refer people, as widely as the post manages to travel, back to your website.

Of course, you won't only be posting your own content. You'll be sharing other people's blog posts and videos that you find interesting and relevant to your audience (of course, with your own comment attached), and you can also share more light-hearted material, such as inspirational stories, quotes or funny videos, that perhaps aren't directly related to your business or your subject matter, but you feel will resonate with people or amuse them.

MAKE YOUR CONTENT WORK FOR YOU

You can post your own content more than once. People are in different time zones all over the world so they're not going to notice every single update you post, plus they read many different people's social media updates, not just yours. So recycling your content, a little down the line and with different introductory text, makes perfect sense.

* An expression often used in marketing that was coined by Bob Burg and John David Mann in their parable *The Go-Giver*, referring to the idea that people prefer to do business with people they know, like, and trust.

INTEGRATING SOCIAL MEDIA
into your website

You'll want to integrate social media in the following ways:

1. Badges that link to the business or owner's profile page. They may look something like this, depending on your website's design (1). These are usually at the top, at the top of the sidebar, or in the bottom area (the footer) of every page.

2. Buttons that allow visitors to "like" or "follow" from the web page you are on, without leaving the page (2a, 2b). These are usually in the sidebar or in the footer.

3. Buttons that allow visitors to share your page or post with their network, without leaving the page (3a; these ones are usually at the top or the bottom of a blog post, 3b; this one floats at the side of the page—you can get one like it by installing SumoMe; see page 161). (Note that you yourself don't actually need to be signed up to the social media platforms for which you display a sharing icon—these buttons are for your site visitors to share your content with their own networks, on whichever social media they like to use themselves.)

4. Put sharing buttons on your images, since images get shared often (4; the buttons appear when the image is moused-over).

It's a good idea to offer all these options to your site visitors. This isn't over-doing it—people expect to be able to easily share and like what they want to.

FACEBOOK PAGES

In order to have people "Like" you on Facebook, you need to set up a Page and not a Profile—that is, representing a company, a brand, a product, a public figure, a local business, etc., rather than a regular individual's Facebook profile.

WHICH SOCIAL MEDIA SHOULD YOU USE?

Don't feel pressured to be active on every social platform, nor rush to investigate the very newest thing, unless this is the kind of thing that really grabs you. The only places you need to be are where your prospective audience is. So first find out where those places are, and start interacting.

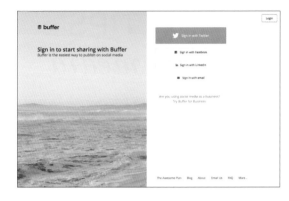

△ Buffer is one of several systems you can use to automate your social media. Since it has a free version, Buffer is a good place to try out automation

HTTPS://BUFFER.COM

As well as these common ways of encouraging people to share, you may also want to embed certain of your feeds into your website—for example, Facebook, Twitter, or Instagram; the latter gives a fun glimpse into what's going on in your life outside the website, and they all give the clear impression that you're busy and in action.

AUTOMATING YOUR SOCIAL MEDIA POSTS

It doesn't make sense to spend hours every day updating your social media—you have a life to lead and most likely a business to run as well. But social media posts can get lost quickly; if you really want to make an impact with social media you need to post often— several times a day, even. One way to do this is to automate your posts. This absolutely doesn't need to feel artificial; you write them all yourself, of course—they just get posted out while you are sleeping, or doing something else, and in addition, if you aim to have global reach, it makes sense to vary the times you post, because of different time-zones.

Here are some useful tools that can automate your posts across the most commonly used social media:

Buffer https://buffer.com
Hootsuite https://hootsuite.com
Edgar http://meetedgar.com
Post Planner http://www.postplanner.com

CLICK TO TWEET

Click To Tweet (https://clicktotweet.com) is a fantastically easy tool that allows you to create a link within your website text that when clicked on, opens a "tweet" box! This makes it as easy as you could ever wish to encourage your site visitors to share your wise words (plus, of course, your website address and Twitter handle; if you need to shorten the web page address to conserve space, you can do this at https://bitly.com).

IDEAS & TIPS
for social media

Social media marketing—the dos and don'ts, the best practices, the specific ways to get the most out of each of the individual platforms—has developed into a massive, specialized area all of its own. Some people take naturally to social media, others find it a challenge—what's undeniable is that it's the most powerful machine there is when it comes to publicizing you and your website, and it totally makes sense to use it. If you're someone who's wary about diving into this huge and relatively new world, here are some basic ways of making social media work for you.

- As we said back in Chapter 6, when we were talking about visuals, posts with images get read and shared more than any other posts. You'll want to act on this and add images whenever you can—as shown opposite, Canva makes this really easy for you by offering you the exact right sizes for the different social media you might want to post to. If your website is product-based, your task is fairly unchallenging. Good visual material you can post, other than the obvious photos of your products, includes pictures of customers enjoying your products, ideas of what you can do with your products, new designs, behind-the-scenes shots, how your products are made, and so on. You can encourage people to interact with you by sending in their own images; perhaps hold a contest for the most bizarre, inventive, artistic, creative, etc. depending on what appeals to you, and might appeal to them.

- But if what you do doesn't easily lend itself to images, all is not lost. Thanks to graphics software like Canva (and some other tools such as Pablo, shown opposite, and some others listed in Chapter 13), it's easy to create attractive images out of statements and quotations. These don't need to relate precisely to what you do—they can flesh out your audience's conception of you, reinforcing the "image" that you want to project. Quotes make great "shareable" content, and you can post them on any of the social media, not only those designed specifically for visuals. (See the image at top-left on the page overleaf for a brilliant example of creativity in an entirely non-visual field).

- Most of us are comfortable with Facebook as we've been using it on a personal level for years. If you're running a business or any kind of organization you'll need to set up a Facebook Page (rather than a profile), as noted in the tip box on page 146, so that people can "Like" you. If your Facebook Page is classified as a Local Business, you can extend its reach to allow people to post ratings and reviews directly to Facebook, which will gain you a lot more traction and act as proof of your popularity. Just add your business address into the Page Info section and save; click the address again and select the checkbox next to "Show map, check-ins and star ratings on the Page."

- Similarly, you can extend the reach of your online store, depending on your platform, right onto Facebook. If you have an online store with Wix or Shopify, you can set up a

△ Canva has the sizes you need all set up and ready for you to make images to post on social media. You can also make ready-sized Facebook covers, Twitter headers, etc.
HTTPS://WWW.CANVA.COM

◁ Pablo's one of a number of easy-to-use online tools you can use to turn a quotation into a ready-sized social media graphic.
HTTPS://BUFFER.COM/PABLO

Facebook app and sell directly from your Facebook page, as in the example shown overleaf. You can also sell on Facebook if you have an Ecwid store; check with your platform as this is an area that's bound to develop.

- Pinterest has shown itself to be a platform that really engages its users, and for this reason, "Rich pins" have been developed, which show details such as recipe ingredients, prices, and stock levels (as shown at bottom-left on the page overleaf), if the original creator of the post has set this up ahead of time. Rich pins are a little tricky to enable at this present time, though you can do it without problems via Shopify and Squarespace. Shopify actually allows you to set up a "Buyable pin" which, more than just showing details, actually allows people to purchase without leaving Pinterest—this is a development which is certain to become more widespread so do ask your platform.
- As we mentioned back in Chapter 7, video is a really great way of communicating with your audience. Periscope one of the newest of the social media (see page 127) and it lets you engage live with people who are interested in what you do. As we said, it doesn't remain live on the Periscope

platform for longer than 24 hours but you can "repurpose" your content and post it to YouTube, and then share it. Don't forget that you can also use it the other way around, to connect with other people whose sphere you'd like to be in; log in to their scopes regularly, ask good questions, and you'll build a relationship.

- To sum up, if you're not really very keen on social media, you only need to make sure you're present and interacting on the platforms where your audience already are. If on the other hand, you really love it, you'll be excited to see how you can use the innovative new platforms that spring up all the time.

ATTACH IMAGES TO SOCIAL MEDIA POSTS WHENEVER POSSIBLE

Posts with images get a lot more shares! This is where tools like Canva come in super-handy.

Internet personality and software startup founder Nathalie Lussier makes on-brand graphics for her Instagram feed, and intersperses them with lifestyle and "behind-the-scenes" shots to give a picture of herself, her company ethos and her company's development.

HTTPS://WWW.INSTAGRAM.COM/NATHLUSSIER/

Integrating your store with Facebook lets customers buy then and there.

HTTPS://WWW.FACEBOOK.COM/ALPHLY/

Facebook's Reviews function

Rich pins provide pricing and stock information, or recipe ingredients, article details, movie information, or geographical location. Ask your platform whether you can easily enable them.

This Italian restaurant has thousands of reviews, and customers can view the menu and make an online reservation directly from Facebook.

HTTPS://WWW.FACEBOOK.COM/RPMITALIAN

DIGITAL PARENTING COACH
SELF-HOSTED WORDPRESS

FRANCE

HTTP://WWW.DIGITALPARENTINGCOACH.COM

"A good website is one where your particular tribe or target audience gets what you are trying to say, appreciate the manner in which you say it and they come back to you again and again because you are a trusted friend. A good website is your digital face, a friendly handshake, a warm hug, a kick in the pants, a glass of wine, a cup of great coffee. A good website may need a bit of tweaking, a bit of polish, so don't think that once it's done, it's done. You can come back to it in a year and see what still works or what doesn't work so that as you evolve or your business evolves, your website evolves to reflect that change.

My biggest challenge was not knowing my target audience before I started. I initially thought my audience would be businesses and organizations, but over time I realized that, in fact, my content resonated for individual parents and caregivers. And one of the best ways to reach out to those people in order to share my advice and resources is via social media, whether that be Facebook, Twitter, Periscope, Blab, Pinterest, or Instagram. Different parents prefer different tools and I love adapting my materials to those tools.

Don't be a perfectionist, be a get-it-done-ist—take it all in your stride and enjoy what you are creating."

Elizabeth Milovidov

11 The *Search Engines*

How the SEARCH ENGINES WORK

The search engines* work using a sorting method called an algorithm. The algorithm changes from time to time so that the search engines can produce the best and most relevant results for the people using them. It's your job as a website owner to indicate as clearly as you can to the search engines what your site is about, so that it can be found by the maximum of people searching for the kind of information, products or service that you offer. The process of preparing your website is called SEO, or "Search Engine Optimization."

*Google is the most widely used search engine, with about 64% of global market share; Yahoo and Bing each have about 10% (although actually Yahoo is powered by Bing). Baidu is the search engine of choice in China, giving it also about 10% of global market share.

There's no cheating the search engines—you can't get away with tricks like hiding keywords in the code, for example—and you can't pay for a good ranking (though of course, you can pay to advertise). Instead, you can prepare your site as best as you can to get the best ranking possible. Let's see how you can do this.

There are a number of factors that determine how the search engines read your website (see the diagram opposite).

1. The wording on your site. The search engines attach a huge amount of importance to the words that appear in the pages of your site, so you need to make sure you include the right keywords in the wording on your website.

2. How much relevant content there is on the site relating to those keywords (here's where your blog content comes in useful).

3. How often you update your site—the search engines love dynamic content that changes often (again, your blog ticks this box).

4. How much traffic your website gets. For the search engines, this is a measure of how "important" your website is, and therefore how highly it should be ranked.

5. How many sites link in to yours. This shows whether your site is seen to be influential and therefore "important" within your niche. This goes hand in hand with how much traffic your site gets.

6. There are some technical considerations to pay attention to as well, which we will look at over the page.

CHOOSING YOUR KEYWORDS

What words would people wanting to find a site like yours type into the search engines? Make a list, and then see what kind of sites come up on the first page in searches for each of these phrases. You want to be on the first page of Google for your chosen keywords—if you anticipate being found this way. If large organizations are listed first, it's unlikely, realistically speaking, that you'll be able to beat these high-ranking, established websites. You have two options if this is the case. You can concentrate on marketing your site in real-world situations, or explore online marketing strategies (see Chapter 12), and bring traffic to your website in other ways than from the search engines. Or you concentrate on keywords that have less competition, for example, if "graphic designer" + "your city" is too competitive, how about trying "graphic designer" + "your area in the city"?

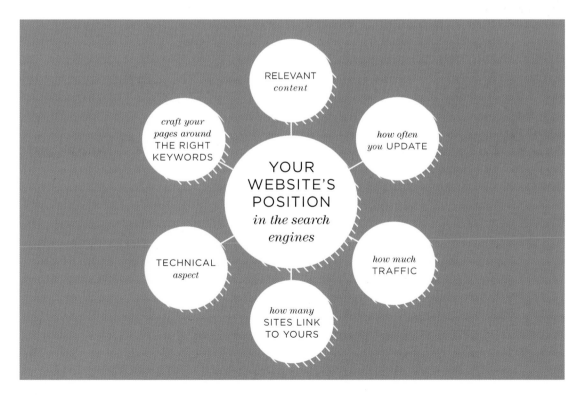

OPTIMIZING YOUR WEBSITE
around your search terms

Once you've decided which keywords and phrases* you're going to build your site around, you need to optimize your site around them.

INCLUDING YOUR SEARCH TERMS IN YOUR PAGE TEXT

You need to make sure you put your keywords and phrases into the text that is on your website pages as this is the most important indication to the search engines as to what your website is about. The largest heading on a page is seen as the most significant—it's more specifically known as an "H1" heading (this is the way it is described in website code, but it's generally known this way as well; don't waste this important position on your home page by saying something like "Welcome to our site!"). The search engines also pay attention to smaller-sized headings in the page, which have a descending hierarchy and carry a corresponding amount of weight.

You should repeat your most important search terms within the text—but at all times remember that your site text is going to be read by real people and if you repeat the keywords too often it's going to come off as "spammy." (Plus you may end up getting penalised by the search engines as well, if this is done in an unnatural way.) If in any doubt, I'd always sacrifice repeating my search terms in favor of the text reading well to the visitors.

*A keyword is a word that someone will use to type into Google to perform a search; a key phrase is simply more than one word—a very common way to search.

PAGE TITLES, DESCRIPTIONS, AND OTHER TECHNICALITIES

As well as crafting the wording of your pages with care and attention, there are a number of technicalities you need to pay attention to.

1. Every platform provides you with a way of specifying the title of each of your web pages (for self-hosted WordPress, use the Yoast SEO plugin.) Page titles are not the same as the headings on your pages. They are the title that appears at the top of your browser window, and in the search engines as the title for your site; see the screenshot opposite. These carry a huge

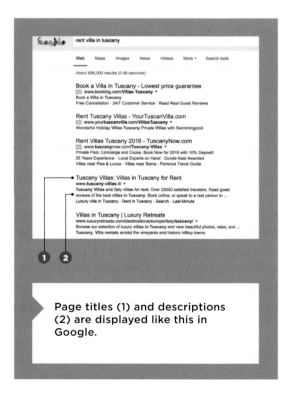

Page titles (1) and descriptions (2) are displayed like this in Google.

importance for the search engines, so you need to be sure the right keywords are in there. It's common practice to put your main keyword first, followed by a "|" or a "-" and then the brand name, website name, or another, slightly less important keyword. You should label the different pages in your site in the same way, with, for example, "FAQ" or "About," depending on the page, before these two elements. Page titles should be no more than 55 characters in length, or they may be cut off.

2. Alongside the facility to add a page title, you'll also have the possibility of adding a description. These descriptions are for humans and can be seen in the search engines, as shown in the screenshot opposite—you don't actually need to put your search terms in here, but it may be logical to do so. You can also add calls to action, phone numbers, dates of sales or of special opening hours, and so on here. If you don't put anything here, the search engines will just take the text on your page, so you're missing out if you don't spend some time thinking about how to craft these descriptions. Your page descriptions shouldn't be longer than 160 characters, again because you risk getting them cut off.

3. Thirdly, think about how you name your images—it makes a difference to the search engines. Before you upload them to your site, rename them in a sensible way that tells the search engines something about your website. For example, villa_tuscany1 .jpg, etc. (Not "IMG_2656.1JPG!"). If your platform gives you the opportunity, there may also be something called an "Alt" field that you can enter information into. Don't worry about the technicalities of this, just add the the same keywords into that field plus something more precise—for example, "villa in tuscany swimming pool."

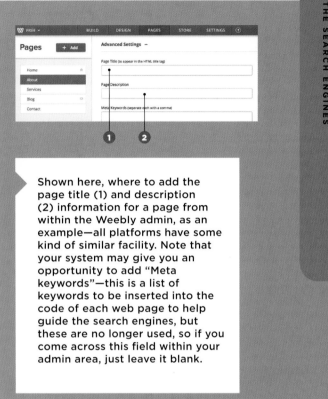

Shown here, where to add the page title (1) and description (2) information for a page from within the Weebly admin, as an example—all platforms have some kind of similar facility. Note that your system may give you an opportunity to add "Meta keywords"—this is a list of keywords to be inserted into the code of each web page to help guide the search engines, but these are no longer used, so if you come across this field within your admin area, just leave it blank.

SUBMITTING TO THE SEARCH ENGINES

Submit your completed site here:
Google: https://www.google.com/webmasters/tools/submit-url
Bing: http://www.bing.com/toolbox/submit-site-url

In conclusion, the best guideline to getting the right people to find you through the search engines is simply to construct the best site that you can, optimize it as above, and concentrate on adding increasing amounts of excellent, relevant material to the site.

12 Promoting *Your Website*

We've looked at blogging, social media, and the search engines—all three very powerful ways of bringing people to your website.

In this chapter we'll look at some of the other ways you can promote your website both on- and offline.

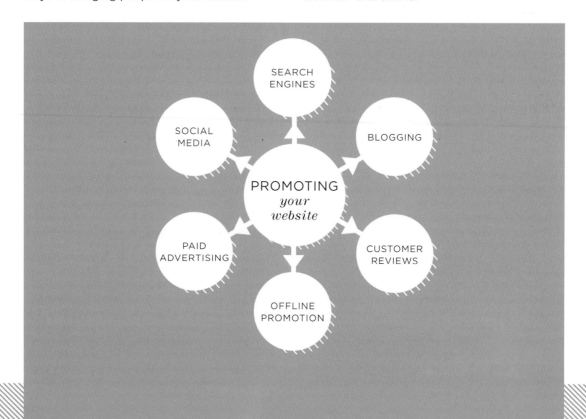

SEARCH ENGINES

SOCIAL MEDIA

BLOGGING

PROMOTING *your website*

PAID ADVERTISING

CUSTOMER REVIEWS

OFFLINE PROMOTION

Pay-per-click ADVERTISING

Pay-per-click advertising—known as "PPC"—can be one of the quickest ways of getting people to your website. Google AdWords is the best known of these networks. It works according to keywords (or key phrases); you choose for which keywords you want your ad to appear, and when someone searches on Google using the keyword or phrase you have specified, your ad appears. You pay each time a prospective customer clicks through to your website. The cost of each click depends on how much competition (between advertisers) there is for that keyword, and you set a daily limit so that you don't go over budget. PPC advertising can be really effective, but it can add up very quickly if you're in any kind of "in-demand" domain; you'll want to set up a "goal" within your Google Analytics account (see page 164) so you can analyze how cost-effective it is for you to advertise this way.

Bing has its own advertising network that works in the same way; you can also advertise on Facebook, Instagram, LinkedIn, and Twitter.

Google AdWords: http://www.google.com/adwords/
Bing Ads: http://advertise.bingads.microsoft.com
Facebook Ads: https://www.facebook.com/business/products/ads/
Instagram Ads: https://business.instagram.com/advertising/
LinkedIn Ads: https://www.linkedin.com/ad/start
Twitter Ads: https://ads.twitter.com

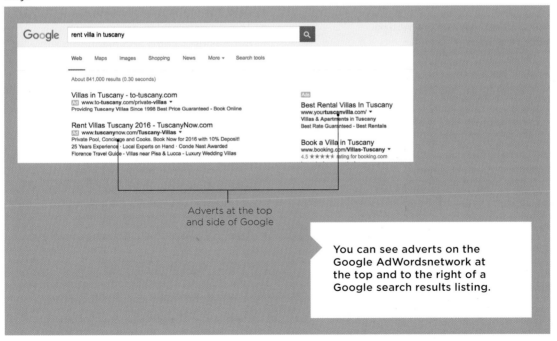

Adverts at the top and side of Google

You can see adverts on the Google AdWordsnetwork at the top and to the right of a Google search results listing.

Customer REVIEWS

Online reviews are an excellent way of promoting your business—people have confidence in unsolicited consumer reviews. If you have a real-world business, here are some places you can encourage your happy customers to place their comments:

TripAdvisor: http://www.tripadvisor.com
Yelp: http://www.yelp.com
Google Business: https://business.google.com/add?service

Trustpilot (for both on- and offline businesses and stores): **https://www.trustpilot.com**

For online stores, you can install review apps; for Wix sites, the Customer Reviews app. For Shopify sites, there are any number of apps you can add including the well-known Yotpo, which sends a follow-up email after a sale that allows the purchaser to reply by email, sends reviews to Facebook and Twitter, and helps you accumulate review stars in Google searches.

Other ways of PROMOTING YOUR SITE

OTHER ONLINE WAYS OF PROMOTING

Some other ways of promoting your website are:

- Paid advertising on other people's websites.
- Getting listed on a portal or an association website. Linking to your website from here should bring you traffic as well as raising up the ranking of your own site.
- Commenting on other people's blogs—again, this is about building relationships rather than barefacedly promoting yourself.
- Getting reviewed, or interviewed, on other people's websites.

OFFLINE PROMOTION

Just because it's a website doesn't mean you need to forget the traditional, real-world ways of promoting and networking among people, face to face.

- Getting press coverage.
- Paid ads in the traditional press.
- Joining networking groups, giving out business cards and meeting people at events.
- Distributing fliers or postcards.
- Giving away stickers (https://www.stickermule.com or http://www.moo.com).
- Giving free demonstrations, talks, or advice sessions.
- Collecting email addresses for your email list at events (either by collecting business cards, asking people to write on a sheet of paper, or by inputting them directly into your email list via a tablet).
- Running giveaways and competitions to grow your list.
- Finally, don't forget to put your website link, plus your social media details, in an email signature at the bottom of every email you send out.

CHILLOUT HOSTEL ZAGREB
STRIKINGLY

CROATIA	HTTP://WWW.CHILLOUT-HOSTEL-ZAGREB.COM

"We wanted to engage the visitor, provide relevant information in the blink of a scroll, and enable the customer to book accommodation quickly and reliably.

The idea was to mirror the experience a customer gets while staying with us. We wanted to present only essential information in a way that would familiarize the visitor with our brand and philosophy.

Carefully decide what and how you want to communicate with the potential customer, just like in real life. Nobody wants to read long texts and spend time navigating the page—this is ancient history. Keep it short, precise, and relevant, engaging and entertaining. Make sure your page "screams" what it's about.

Be prepared to test and question what works and what doesn't. In most cases, what you believe is nice or relevant and should be featured on your web site, most likely isn't. Put yourself in your customer's shoes and outline the site in a way you as a customer would enjoy and find useful. I must point out that the platform is one of the best we have seen to this day and it is impressive how well it works."

Mislav Becejac

13 Tools & Extras

Tools for SPECIFIC PURPOSES

THE SIMPLEST WEB PRESENCE POSSIBLE
If you need to get something up extremely fast, About.me can provide a simple page with a photo, your name and your contact/social media details—a useful stop-gap while you're figuring out your site-building options. Of course, you should connect it to your own domain to remove their branding, even if it's a temporary solution:

https://about.me

LANDING PAGES
Landing pages—also known as "squeeze pages"—are pages on your site (or on a subdomain) that are designed to do just one specific job, most usually collect an email address in return for a free giveaway, but they can also be used to encourage a site visitor to click through to make a purchase or sign up for

a trial, or register for a webinar. A landing page has as few distractions as possible and doesn't include links out to the rest of the site, so as to increase the chance of gathering the email address of the visitor, or whatever the specific aim of the page is.

A landing page can be used as a "Coming Soon" page, and is a great way of capturing visitors' email addresses while you're working on your main website. There are a number of tools that let you make super-professional landing pages with just a few clicks:

https://instapage.com
http://www.leadpages.net
http://unbounce.com

These systems are compatible with most email list providers, and integrate with WordPress. If you're using WordPress, note that certain themes, for example Divi, pictured on page 105, have a built-in landing page option meaning you can create a page that fits in with the look of the rest of the site, and this can be quite a big money-saver if you have several landing pages to create.

LIST-BUILDING & TRAFFIC-BUILDING TOOLS

SumoMe is a fantastically useful suite of tools that work on all platforms. List-building tools include a signup popup that you can configure to appear how often you want, and after how long a visitor has been on your site, a bar at the top of your site with a newsletter signup in it (or a "call to action" button—"Click here," "Get it," etc.), a full-screen "welcome mat" signup popup, and a signup form that appears at the bottom of your screen after readers have finished reading blog posts.

Social media tools include those "share" buttons that are shown at the side of the web pages you're browsing, and image sharing buttons to make it easy for people to pass them on (as we know, images get shared more than any other type of content). Other popular free tools are a heat map—a content analysis tool that shows you which parts of your long pages people are actually reading—and a contact form that sends the person contacting you an automatic message. This is a suite of tools I really recommend you get—and all these features at basic level are free:

https://sumome.com

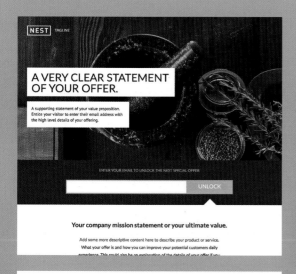

Landing pages can be used to collect email addresses or as a "Coming soon" page. The one shown here is the Nest template from Unbounce.

HTTP://UNBOUNCE.COM
Unbounce-designed template used with permission.

A popup signup form, like this one powered by SumoMe (here shown on their own website), can have a huge impact on your subscriber numbers.

HTTPS://SUMOME.COM

ONLINE COMPETITIONS

One of the best ways of growing your list is by running an online contest. This tool is designed especially to help you do that:

http://contestdomination.com

WEBINARS

http://www.webinarjam.com
https://www.webinarsonair.com
http://www.clickwebinar.com
http://www.gotomeeting.com/webinar
http://webinarninja.co

SendOwl is a popular way of managing the sale and delivery of digital products. The system can integrate with your email list service, drip feed content to your purchasers, and handle video streaming (so that customers don't have to wait for a huge video to download before beginning watching).

HTTPS://WWW.SENDOWL.COM

ONLINE COURSES & MEMBERSHIP SITES

https://zippycourses.com
https://www.coursecraft.net
https://teachable.com
https://www.kajabiapp.com
https://www.teachery.co

DIGITAL DOWNLOAD DELIVERY

https://www.sendowl.com
http://www.e-junkie.com
https://gumroad.com
http://pulleyapp.com
https://sellfy.com
http://getdpd.com
http://www.fetchapp.com

ONLINE SCHEDULING SOFTWARE

Allow customers to book their own appointments with you:

https://www.vcita.com
http://www.timetrade.com
http://www.appointy.com
https://acuityscheduling.com

LIVE CHAT

https://www.zopim.com
http://www.livechatinc.com
https://www.clickdesk.com
https://www.purechat.com
https://www.olark.com

PODCAST HOSTING

http://www.podbean.com
https://www.podomatic.com
https://www.buzzsprout.com
https://www.spreaker.com
http://www.libsyn.com

ORDER FULFILLMENT
Taking care of order fulfillment from your online store:

http://services.amazon.com/content/
fulfillment-by-amazon.htm
http://www.shipwire.com
http://www.webgistix.com
(now called Rakuten)

COMMENTS/DISCUSSION

https://disqus.com

FORMS
(For example, if you're building a site on Strikingly and you need more information from your site visitors than their form can gather, you can either copy and paste the embed code into an HTML box or use the app store.)

http://www.wufoo.com
http://www.typeform.com
https://www.formstack.com
https://www.google.com/forms/about/

EVENTS
Sell tickets and manage reservations online:

https://www.eventbrite.com

DISPLAYING VIDEOS
Group videos into galleries:

https://huzzaz.com

MULTI-LINGUAL WEBSITE BUILDER

http://www.voog.com

IDENTIFYING WORDPRESS THEMES
Tool to show what theme and what plugins a site is using:

http://whatwpthemeisthat.com/

KEEP UPDATED
Keep your eye on the resources section of my website http://www.alannahmoore.com. New tools appear all the time, replacing those that become outdated, and I'll list them for you there.

ONLINE QUOTE-MAKERS
Make images from quotations:

https://getstencil.com/
https://buffer.com/pablo

RESOURCES FOR MAKING YOUR OWN GRAPHICS:

http://subtlepatterns.com
http://thepatternlibrary.com
http://www.colourlovers.com
http://inspirationhut.net/blurgrounds/
https://www.iconfinder.com
https://thenounproject.com

SOCIAL MEDIA PHOTO RESIZER

http://www.internetmarketingninjas.com/
seo-tools/favicon-generator-crop-images/

EMAIL MARKETING FOR BLOGGERS

http://convertkit.com

Tracking your TRAFFIC *& your* SITE PERFORMANCE

Your website-building system may give you a stats area so you can see how much traffic you are getting (people visiting your site), where they are coming from (if they've come from Google, if they've come from another website where someone has written about you, or if they've come directly to your website), and when your visitors are coming (at the weekend, in the evenings, as a result of a particular promotion, and so on). As your traffic increases, though, it's likely that these fairly simple statistics aren't going to satisfy your appetite to understand better how your website is working—after all, it's logical to want to know what's working on your site so that you can do more of it, and cut out what isn't working.

GOOGLE ANALYTICS

For more detailed analysis of your stats, Google Analytics (https://www.google.com/analytics/) is the undisputed way to go. You need a Google account to get set up, and then you need to create an account for your website within Google Analytics. How exactly you hook up Google Analytics to your site depends on your platform; you'll find instructions for each system as to how to do this. (With WordPress you'll need a plugin—Google Analytics by Yoast).

Google Analytics will provide you with as many stats as you'll ever need. The interface is complex since it provides you with so much information—if you want to understand this information in more detail you may want to

TESTING DIFFERENT VARIABLES

You may want to test different versions of your site to see which gets better results. Optimizely lets you tweak your website so that it works as well as it possibly can, and you can use it with all of the major platforms, including Strikingly.

HTTPS://WWW.OPTIMIZELY.COM

look at some of their training videos, however a simpler system is to install the SumoMe plugin which provides you with an easy way to understand what you're seeing as it applies to each page (http://www.appsumo.com/google-analytics-sumome/).

One thing you will probably want to do within the Google Analytics admin area is to set up some "goals." A goal, for example, could be someone signing up for your newsletter, or it could be making a purchase. To find out the basics of this, click on "Conversions" > "Goals" > "Overview" and watch the video.

You'll also be able to see from within Google Analytics which keywords are bringing visitors to your site from Google, and which of the social media are having an impact on your traffic—and your goals.

GOOGLE SEARCH CONSOLE

As well as understanding more about your site visitors, you'll probably want to check that your site is being listed correctly in Google. Here's where Google Search Console (https://www.google.com/webmasters/tools/) comes in (it used to be called Google Webmaster Tools—you may see it referred to this way in some places, but it's the same thing). Your platform will give you instructions as to how to connect; for self-hosted WordPress, you can connect via your Yoast SEO plugin, using the "Webmaster Tools" tab.

Google Search Console allows you to access all kinds of Google-related stats, but most people will need it for two reasons. Firstly, to submit a sitemap to Google. A sitemap is a plan of your site in code—it isn't for visitors; it's to ensure that Google can see and list all the pages on your site so that each time you add a new page, Google will know that it needs to be "crawled." Your platform will automatically generate a sitemap for you—the address of the sitemap is usually something like http://www.yourdomain.com/sitemap.xml—and you can then submit it to Google Search Console (go to Crawl > Sitemaps, then click the "Add/Test Sitemaps" button to the right). For self-hosted WordPress, use the Google XML Sitemaps plugin to generate a sitemap.

Secondly, if Google isn't listing your site correctly, you can request a crawl. Go to Crawl > Fetch as Google and type the page you want to have crawled in the field (leave it blank if you want the site crawled from the home page). Click "Fetch;" when you see "Complete," you can click the "Submit to index" button and select the radio button marked "Crawl this URL and its direct links," then click "Go."

Bing also has its set of tools for data analysis: go to http://www.bing.com/toolbox/webmaster and connect in the same way as you did for Google Search Console.

TRACKING YOUR LINKS ON SOCIAL MEDIA

We mentioned Bitly very briefly on page 147 as an invaluable way of shortening long website links for Twitter. If you sign up for an account (free), it's also a brilliant way of seeing how many clicks your links are getting when you post them on social media—and anywhere else (guest blog posts, etc.).

HTTPS://BITLY.COM

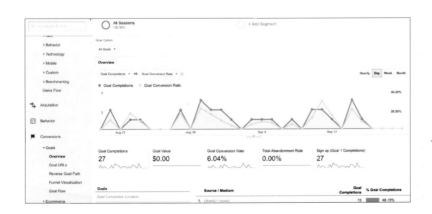

◁ Google Analytics can show you the conversion rate of your website visitors concerning a certain "goal"—shown here, signing up to a newsletter.

INSTAGRAM TOOLS

There are quite a few fun apps you can use to add wording and doodles to your Instagram photos—these can be used to make really nice-looking sidebar badges for your website, instead (save them to your camera roll, email them to yourself, resize if necessary and upload them to your site). Here are just some of these brilliant tools:

http://www.redcact.us/#instaquote
(iOS/Android)
http://wordswag.co
(iOS-only—at the time of writing)
http://www.abeautifulmessapp.com
(iOS/Android)
http://madewithover.com
(iOS-only—at the time of writing)

◁ These tools, which are really made for Instagram
△ images, are fantastic for making square images that link to pages or posts on your website.

PLUGINS *for* *self-hosted WordPress*

There are so many hundreds of WordPress plugins to choose from that it can be a little daunting deciding which ones to use. This list may help you, but remember, things change all the time; the easiest way to find out which plugins are the current best is simply to Google "best WordPress plugin for membership site," for example, and check through the most recent articles that come up. You can install all these plugins by searching them from within the "Plugins" area of your WordPress admin.

UpdraftPlus—you must, repeat absolutely must, get a backup system in place for your site (separate from any backups your host does for you). This plugin (among several others) allows you to automatically save backups to your Dropbox.

Akismet—a necessity, to protect you from comment spam. You really need it! The plugin comes pre-installed, but you need a code to activate it. For a non-personal site, you have to pay; the price you pay is (at the time of writing) up to you. (The plugin was developed by the makers of WordPress, which is why you can log into Akismet with a WordPress.com account, if you have one.)

Yoast SEO—the current favorite SEO plugin for WordPress.

Contact Form 7—this is the most-used contact form, however you have other options: the Jetpack plugin has a contact form, your theme may have a built-in contact form, and there's also the contact form by SumoMe you can use. Make sure you test your contact form regularly to make sure it's working.

Jetpack—a suite of tools that WordPress.com and self-hosted WordPress users can use. (The latter need to sign up with a WordPress.com username, which you can get on the spot if you haven't already got one.) Some of the most useful tools in this bundle are the visibility button for widgets, making it easy to control which widgets appear on which page, the widget that lets you put images in the sidebar, and the gallery carousel which is great if your theme doesn't have a fancy-looking gallery slideshow feature. New tools get added all the time, so you'll have some fun browsing around once you've installed it, and seeing what's available.

Google Analytics (by Yoast)—connect with Google Analytics (see page 164). You'll be able to see some of your results from within the admin area.

Google XML Sitemaps—builds a sitemap that helps the search engines index your site. (This is not for humans, just for robots.)

Email Address Encoder—protect your email address (which you will want to show on your contact page) from harvesters (robots that collect unprotected email addresses on websites, in order to spam them).

Events Manager—this is a very complete but tricky to set up events calendar. You may prefer the more straightforward Events Calendar (by Modern Tribe).

MailChimp List Subscribe Form—this is one of several MailChimp plugins that allow you to have slightly more control over the way the form appears on your site.

PopupAlly—free and premium versions. This is, at the time of writing, the best way of getting a signup form in a strip that runs right across your website, unless you're smart enough to have chosen a theme that offers you this, already integrated.

WP Google Maps—to include a map in your site, if your theme doesn't have this built-in.

Coming Soon (by SeedProd)—this is a nice holding page plugin that lets you put a logo and even a signup form. A dead simple one is Under Construction, if you prefer.

My Post Order—this is useful if you want to order your posts other than chronologically.

NextGEN Gallery—allows you to arrange your photos into albums, which unless you've got a special photography or portfolio theme that allows you to do that, you wouldn't normally be able to do.

Sell Media—sell prints (e.g. photography) and downloads.

Easy Digital Downloads—free, but with several premium add-ons that can make your sell/download flow more professional. One of the most popular ways of selling digital products via WordPress. (You don't need to have a full e-commerce theme, which you would if you were using WooCommerce, which also handles digital downloads.)

Sensei—premium plugin from WooThemes for delivering online courses.

WPML (premium), Polylang (free, and easier to set up)—to run multi-lingual sites.

WishList—for membership sites

http://wishlistproducts.com

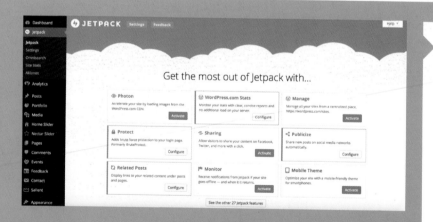

The Jetpack bundle, provided by the makers of WordPress, grows all the time to include all kinds of features from extra security and social media sharing to extra sidebar widgets and a "Post by email" feature.

HTTP://JETPACK.ME

MAMA LOVES PARIS
SELF-HOSTED WORDPRESS

| FRANCE | HTTP://MAMALOVESPARIS.COM |

"At first glance it feels like you are going into the cockpit of a helicopter with no flying experience, but if you go through the process step by step, explore the theme, and follow instructions, you can end up being a semi-pro in no time.

Choose your theme wisely. Consider what design really suits your aesthetic and how you will be able to adapt it to suit your needs.

Balance is everything—combine your words with pictures in a way that will amplify your story. Images create impact and help retain interest in your posts.

Plugins make it dynamic. Use plug-ins to add fun dimensions to your site. From social media to news feeds, they help keep the site fresh and up to date.

Once you have created your fabulous site, work hard at marketing it. Use social media to get your message out there. Select the platforms that are best for you and work diligently to build an audience. Each social media channel has different benefits—once identified, deliver your brand voice with impact. It will take time, but it's worth it."

Claudette Parry Laws

14 *Important* Things to Know

Before you go live with your site, you need to consider some legal matters that will probably impact you; you may need to look into these in some detail, or get professional advice, since the rules vary according to where you are based in the world.

LEGALITIES

PCI COMPLIANCE

The Payment Card Industry Data Security Standard (PCI DSS) is a set of requirements that ensures that all credit card data is stored, processed or transmitted within a secure environment. If you're selling online you need to make sure your payment process meets with these requirements. Using Ecwid, Gumroad, Shopify, Weebly, Wix, or Squarespace, is completely safe; if using WooCommerce you're also within the rules if you use the Mijireh

Checkout plugin (http://www.mijireh.com/woocommerce/). For any other system, you need to check that it's PCI-compliant because if it's not, you could risk a fine. For more information, see here:

https://www.pcisecuritystandards.org/merchants/

https://www.pcicomplianceguide.org.

Or simply check with your payment processor!

PRIVACY

The law dictates, in most countries, that if you collect information from your website visitors (for example, their names and email addresses), you need to state on your website that you will safeguard this information, and any other information gathered, and not share it with a third party. Different countries have different specifications as to what you need to declare publicly, so check this out in detail according to where you are based. US guidelines:

https://www.sba.gov/blogs/7-considerations-crafting-online-privacy-policy

COOKIES

The "EU cookie law" affects you if you are in the EU, or if you deal with anyone in the EU. It decrees that you need to publish a statement allowing users to opt in or out of the use of cookies when browsing a particular website; you have probably already come across these notices. (Cookies are files stored on a user's computer that a web page uses to determine what should be shown on that web page, for example prices may appear in euros, rather than dollars, if the user is in the eurozone.) Some systems—Shopify and WordPress.com, for example—have built-in cookie-alert notices; if you're using self-hosted WordPress there are a number of plugins you can choose from. Failing an existing system on the platform you're using, you may simply be able to publish a clearly visible statement declaring that the website uses cookies, and that continuing to browse the website assumes acceptance;

include a link to a page where you detail what cookies are used. Ask your platform for guidance, and research further, remembering that each country has adapted their laws slightly differently to comply. For UK information, see here:

https://ico.org.uk/for-organisations/guide-to-pecr/cookies-and-similar-technologies/

EMAIL

You've probably heard of the CAN-SPAM laws, designed to curb unsolicited commercial email. These are not hard to comply with, and the chances are that if you're using one of the commercial email mailing list managers, you're already within the law. The rules are basically:

- **Never add anyone to your list without their permission. (You are allowed to add past customers, if you find this appropriate.)**
- **Your message needs to show the name of the person or business that sent the email, a valid email address, and the physical address of the business.**
- **You may not use a misleading subject line.**
- **If you're sending an advertisement rather than an update, you need to make this clear.**
- **You need to let people know how they can unsubscribe from your list, and honor these requests promptly. (Your mailing list manager will do this for you automatically.)**

For more precise details, see this link:

https://www.ftc.gov/tips-advice/business-center/guidance/can-spam-act-compliance-guide-business

---

Privacy & Cookies: This site uses cookies from WordPress.com and selected partners.

To find out more, as well as how to remove or block these, see here: Our Cookie Policy

Close and accept

△ This is the standard cookie statement on a WordPress.com site. (If you set it up as a widget, it will appear at the bottom of the page, and will disappear when clicked on.)

DISCLOSURE OF AFFILIATE LINKS

Guidelines published by the FTA state that if you're reviewing or recommending a product and you receive any financial compensation for doing so, you must clearly declare this (and this shouldn't be at the end, or in a separate "Disclosures" page). This includes affiliate payments—a percentage you get paid if a viewer clicks on a link on your web page and then buys the product. For more information, see here:

https://www.ftc.gov/sites/default/files/attachments/press-releases/ftc-publishes-final-guides-governing-endorsements-testimonials/091005revisedendorsementguides.pdf

TRADEMARKS AND COPYRIGHT

Every country has its own rules regarding copyright and registering. It really pays to research trademarks before you start your business online, just in case you accidentally tread on someone else's toes and end up paying a fine. Concerning copyright, note that you don't have to display a copyright symbol on your website to protect your logo or your artworks, but if you do, it expresses your copyright authority more officially; it isn't usually complicated or expensive to register copyright, so this gives you even more legal weight should a dispute ever arise. If you're US-based, these links may be useful:

http://www.copyright.gov

http://www.uspto.gov/

BUSINESS PERMITS, FISCAL RESPONSIBILITIES, ETC.

Each country (and each state within the US) has different requirements as to what taxes you need to charge your customers, whether you need a business permit, what records you need to keep, and so on; these need to be researched to make sure you're within the law. In addition, if you're doing business with other countries, you need to make sure you comply with international trade laws:

http://www.hg.org/trade.html

EU VAT RULE ON DOWNLOADABLE PRODUCTS

The rules state that if you're selling digital goods—ebooks, online courses, music, videos and software (but not gift cards or coupons sent by email)— to customers in the EU, you need to charge VAT based on your customers' location, rather than your own. Since VAT rates vary from country to country within the EU, this causes some complications, and it may also change the way you are registered for VAT. Your platform and/or your payment processor may have you covered, but you need to check, and in addition, you should ascertain with your tax office whether it impacts your registration, as this will vary according to where you are based. See here for more information:

http://ec.europa.eu/taxation_customs/taxation/

Glossary

Admin area The part of your website that you log into, where you build and make changes; these are then visible to the public on the live part of the site.

App An add-on, sometimes paid-for, usually created by a third party, that you can add to your website to make it perform extra functions (for example adding an online store with Ecwid, or a Woofoo form).

Browser The software you use to surf the internet (e.g. Chrome, Internet Explorer, Firefox, Safari).

CMS Content Management System; a system that allows you to add content to a website without going into the code (i.e. all the systems talked about in this book).

DNS Domain Name System; see "Name servers."

Domain name The address of your website, e.g. www.mywebsite.com.

Extension This usually means the ".com" or ".co.uk" (for example) part of a domain name (see "TLD"). It can also mean an extra that you can add on, for example, we talk about WooCommerce "extensions," meaning premium add-ons that make the software perform extra functions.

Footer The bottom part of your website, in which you commonly put your copyright details; this part may also include widgets.

Front end/back end The live part of your website that the public sees, as distinct from the admin area (also called the "back office"), which is invisible to the public.

FTP File Transfer Protocol; a way of uploading files to your website directly (not via the admin area). You may come across this term, but you will not usually need to upload anything this way.

Header The top part of your website; includes the logo and may also include an image.

Host/hosting company The company that "rents" you space on which to construct your website in cyberspace.

Hosted platform A system that includes your hosting, meaning that you don't need to set up hosting with a separate hosting company. All the platforms talked about in this book, apart from self-hosted WordPress, are "hosted."

Hosted webstore An online store that is hosted for you (e.g. Shopify), as distinct from an online store set up with self-hosted WordPress, for which you need hosting from a hosting company.

HTML Hypertext Markup Language; the basic programming language used to build websites (you will not need to learn this).

Internet merchant account A bank account in which you can deposit sums taken from online sales.

Menu The sequence of links that the visitor clicks on to move around the website.

Name servers The "address" of your web host that you give to your domain name so that it can display your website. This is sometimes a string of numbers; it will be provided to you by your hosting company or your website building platform.

Navigation See "Menu."

Payment gateway A service that authorizes credit card payments and sends the payment to an internet merchant account.

Payment processor An all-in-one system that allows you to take payment online (avoiding the need for a payment gateway and an individual internet merchant account).

Platform The system that you use to build your website e.g. Weebly, self-hosted WordPress, WordPress.com, Shopify, etc.

Registrar The company from which you "purchased" your domain name.

Sidebar A column to the right or left side of a web page in which you can put widgets or other content.

Slider A rectangular area, usually towards the top of the home page, that displays a sequence of rotating images.

Subdomain A subdivision of your domain name, for example, blog.yourdomain.com, a tidy way of "attaching" a blog hosted elsewhere to your main website.

Theme A template—the pre-designed structure around which you will build your site and add your content.

TLD Top Level Domain e.g. ".com" or ".co.uk;" see "Extension."

URL Uniform Resource Locator; the web address of a website, or of a particular page on a site.

Web host See "Host."

Widget an element usually displayed in a sidebar or a footer, such as a Facebook Like button, latest blog posts, or latest tweets.

Index

How to get PROFESSIONAL HELP *with your website*

Creating your own website might turn out, after all, not to be your thing. Or you may want to develop your online business into something more complicated, and you need a designer or developer to work with you. Here are some places you can go to find a professional with the knowledge you need.

For WordPress, if you get stuck, you may find the answers you need at the WordPress.org support forum (https://wordpress.org/support/), on the WordPress FAQ page (https://codex.wordpress.org/FAQ) or simply by Googling your problem—the chances are, someone's already run into the same problem as you, and has found the solution. Failing a DIY solution, you'll be able to find a good developer at any of the links to the right.

Some of the platforms provide you with a list of developers. If you need a WooCommerce expert, try here: http://www.woothemes.com/affiliated-woo-workers/. For Squarespace specialists, try here: http://specialists.squarespace.com; get a quote from a Wix professional here: http://arena.wix.com.

Some good places to find freelance professionals who specialize in any particular platform are:

https://www.upwork.com
https://www.freelancer.com
http://directory.codepoet.com/
(WordPress developers)

Acknowledgments

During the course of writing this book I met and corresponded with dozens of individuals and small business owners all over the world who built their own websites. It's been a real pleasure to interact with you—to hear your stories and learn about the difficulties you encountered and the solutions you found; thank you to each and every one of you for the time and energy you put in to talk with me, and for letting me use your websites as examples. My thanks also to the owners of the various website-building platforms and internet tools who offered help and encouragement. Finally, thank you to my editors at Ilex—Zara Larcombe and Rachel Silverlight—for helping me bring this book into being, and to Elizabeth Milovidov and Laura Hodgson for valuable input along the way.